# THE KOREA KNOT

# THE

## A MILITARY–

Philadelphia

# KOREA KNOT

POLITICAL HISTORY

REVISED EDITION

by

Carl Berger

University of Pennsylvania Press

7471
Printed in the United States of America

To Sylvia

# Preface

THE SOVIET periphery extends in a giant arc from the cold waters of the Baltic down through Eastern Europe to the Black Sea, and across the continent of Asia to the isolated Far Eastern port of Vladivostok and Sakhalin Island. During the years after World War II the nations abutting this great Russian frontier were beset by tension and crisis. However, it was in Germany and Korea in particlular that major clashes of the cold war took place between the Soviet Union, which sought to drive American power from Europe and Asia, and the United States, which sought to contain Russian expansionism.

In Europe the Americans took the lead in the late 1940's in the formation of a Western coalition aimed at halting Communist penetration beyond those Eastern and Central European borders where the Red army halted. The resultant clash of interests almost brought about a new war over blockaded Berlin. However, the first Berlin crisis abated in 1949 when the Russians backed away from armed intervention.

In Asia a different pattern emerged. There the West was weak and the Soviet Union, encouraged by the tremendous Chinese Communist victory over the Chiang Kai-shek forces and by a retrenching United States, decided to experiment with overt action in Korea. Because of that decision, and the subsequent American reaction and Chinese Communist intervention, the history of the world was changed, perhaps decisively.

7

The story of Korea, however, is much more than the Soviet experiment in peninsular war, or the war itself. Its tap roots are deeply embedded in events which occurred years before, some of the n relating to Soviet and American military-political decisions made during World War II. Neither Moscow nor Washington, it is clear, foresaw what bitter consequences would follow those decisions.

In preparing this narrative, my primary purpose has been to uncover the origins of the Korean tragedy, to relate the basic sequence of events as they involved the United States, and to place the war in its proper historical context. The bulk of the research for the volume was conducted at the Library of Congress, Washington, D.C., and at the libraries of Drake University, Des Moines, and the State University of Iowa, Iowa City. Some useful data also was located at the Kokusai Bunka Shinkokai Library, Tokyo, Japan, and at the Korean National Library, Seoul, Korea.

I would like to express my special appreciation to Professor Frank Rosenthal, formerly of Drake University, for his invaluable suggestions and guidance; and to Allan Hoschar, former city editor of the *Des Moines Register,* who aided me in my initial studies.

CARL BERGER

*Washington, D.C.*

# Note on the Second Edition

SINCE I completed work on this volume eight years ago, many important events have taken place relating to Korea, so that a new edition seemed desirable. My main objective in preparing a second edition has been to bring the book up to date. This has involved adding three new chapters to the earlier narrative, covering major governmental changes in South Korea, the failures of the armistice agreement of 1953, and the impact of the Sino-Soviet dispute on the Communist regime in Pyongyang. The final chapter has been completely revised to incorporate some new considerations on the significance of Korea to the continuing cold war. The expanded narrative now covers a twenty year period beginning in 1943, when the United States first became intimately involved in Korean affairs. The bibliography also has been updated, and the index has been completely reworked and reset to cover the new material.

CARL BERGER

*February 1964*
*Washington, D.C.*

# Contents

11

# THE KOREA KNOT

# 1

## Korea's Past:
## A Brief Introduction

THE FOUNTAINHEAD of Korea's tragedy, like that of ancient Palestine or modern Poland, has been her geographic emplacement. Located at a crossroads of Asiatic empires, Korea has been the scene of repeated invasions and encroachments by her stronger neighbors—in modern times, China, Russia, and Japan. Hers is a sad history of a nation whose destiny time after time has been molded by others.

A mountainous peninsula projecting out of the Manchurian land mass, Korea is the striking country which became known to nineteenth-century Western visitors as the "Land of the Morning Calm." In prehistoric times the peninsula may have been the route taken by some early ancestors of the Japanese, who crossed the narrow Korea Strait to settle on the island of Kyushu. It is probable that the Koreans have origins among some unknown postneolithic Asian tribesmen, who migrated into the peninsula four to five thousand years ago.

The Koreans themselves attribute their nation's founding to a semimythical figure, Ki-ja, who reportedly brought early Chinese culture to Korea about 1122 B.C. The nation's recorded history dates from 57 B.C., when the tribes of Korea were organizing themselves into three kingdoms which waged sporadic warfare with one another. These wars continued off and on for some seven hundred years, until one of the kingdoms, Silla, aided by the T'ang dynasty of China, subdued her enemies and unified the country.

China began playing an important role in peninsular events almost from the dawn of Korean history. It was through China that Buddhism came to Korea and, later, Chinese patterns of thought and culture, especially the classical literature of Confucius, had great impact on Korea's development. Beginning with the T'ang dynasty, the Chinese for the first time asserted a claim of suzerainty over Korea. They did this by teaching successfully the Confucian ideal of the father-son relationship between states. The Koreans, in acknowledgment of their debt and the superiority of the Chinese state, paid their obeisance.[1] For a thousand years thereafter, until 1895, this relationship was generally observed. During that lengthy period, when occasion demanded it, the Koreans were forced—sometimes by armed expeditions—to repeat obeisance to China by payment of tribute. But Chinese control was nominal, aimed at perpetuating a form of military alliance and insuring Korea's eternal loyalty to China, or to whoever was ruling China.

Once united by Silla, Korea entered a period of peace lasting nearly three hundred years, during which time a high culture flowered. Silla subsequently was succeeded by the kingdom of Koryu, from which the name Korea was derived. During Koryu's last two centuries, beginning about 1230 A.D., the Mongols, who had conquered China and spilled over into eastern Europe, repeatedly invaded Korea and finally subjugated it. Their new overlords subjected the Koreans to manpower levies for Kublai Khan's unsuccessful attempts to conquer Japan, in 1273 and 1282.

[1] For an excellent discussion of this relationship, see M. Frederick Nelson, *Korea and the Old Orders in Eastern Asia* (Baton Rouge: Louisiana State University Press, 1946), pp. 11-20.

These invasion threats only served to arouse the Japanese and, in the century that followed, the Koreans and Chinese found themselves waging unremitting warfare against Japanese piracy and attacks against coastal areas.

In 1392 an internal revolt led by a Korean general named Yi T'agejo was successful in overthrowing the reigning Korean ruler. Yi proceeded to establish his own dynasty (which was to remain in power into the twentieth century), erecting his capital on the site of the present city of Seoul. Two hundred years later, the Japanese, under the dreaded warlord Hideyoshi, embarked in 1592 on their first Korean campaign to conquer the world (i.e., China). Since the Koreans' military arts had languished in peace, the Japanese were initially victorious and Korea appealed to her ancient Chinese ally for aid. China soon sent her armies to the peninsula.

Seven devastating years of warfare, interspersed by truce talks, followed before the unsuccessful conquerors finally withdrew to Japan, upon Hideyoshi's death, leaving Korea in ruins and exhaustion. Three decades later, in 1627, the unhappy Koreans suffered another invasion, this time by the Manchus, the destined rulers of China. Battered Korea was forced to recognize Manchu sovereignty.

As a result of the three catastrophic invasions (by Mongols, Japanese, and Manchus), the Koreans, to bind up their wounds, retreated into national isolation. For more than two hundred years, beginning about 1630, they fended off contacts with the outside world, earning for their country the sobriquet, "The Hermit Kingdom." Western vessels which attempted to find haven in Korean waters were attacked and sometimes burned. Western missionaries were sought out and slain.

Unfortunately, instead of balm this isolation proved to be another calamity for Korea, for it stopped the clock of

Korean history at a time when the industrial revolution was taking place in Europe. While Korea, and indeed all of Asia, stagnated, the Europeans with their cannon and modern implements were sailing and conquering in the four corners of the world. Only one Asiatic nation immediately recognized the importance of Western science and techniques. Japan, which itself had been aroused out of a long feudal slumber by Commodore Matthew C. Perry's fleet in 1853, embarked upon a feverish program of modernization and industrialization.

Within twenty years the Japanese program had been so successful that Japan, emulating the Western world, began to seek out trade concessions, first with neighboring Korea. Although rebuffed by the Koreans Japan persisted, and in 1875 her opportunity arose following a Korean attack upon a Japanese gunboat in Korean waters. Japan first took her complaint of the attack to China, Korea's ostensible overlord. She found that the Middle Kingdom, grown feeble and corrupt, and splintering under the impact of the West, refused responsibility for Korea's affairs. The Japanese promptly undertook direct negotiations with Korea and, on February 26, 1876, they managed to wring a trade treaty from the Koreans, the first in Korea's history.

Korea's modern period can be said to stem from the signing of the Japanese treaty and becomes an integral part of the story of Japan's efforts to detach the peninsula entirely from its ancient dependency on China. In the years that followed the treaty of 1876, and before the United States first appeared on the scene with a treaty obtained in 1882, Japan made significant progress in infiltrating the peninsula. To Western eyes, it seemed Japan had brought an aura of modern efficiency to Korea, whose society, according to one observer, appeared overburdened by:

. . . a total absence of justice, the insecurity of all earnings, a Government which has carried out the worst traditions on which all unreformed Oriental Governments are based, a class of official robbers steeped in intrigue, a monarch enfeebled by the seclusion of the palace seraglio, the mutual jealousies of interested foreigners, and an all-pervading and terrorizing superstition . . .[2]

The Japanese program for Korea was favored by most Westerners, including an American missionary-educator, Homer B. Hulbert, a friend of Korea and editor of *The Korea Review,* which was to comment:

As everyone knows, Japan desires to see the Korean government established on a progressive basis and to be administered in such a manner that the people shall have the greatest incentive to industry and enterprise, for in this way alone can the resources of the country be developed both for Korea's good and Japan's as well. . . . It should be no small consideration with thinking men that what will conduce to Japanese interests in Korea will also conduce to the welfare of the Korean people themselves.[3]

Japanese activities soon began to affect Korean society, leading in the 1880's to the growth of a progressive movement. Some of the younger Koreans, imbued with ideas of progress, believed the Japanese program would bring a change for the better. However, they faced strong opposition from the Korean conservatives surrounding the throne, who were in turn supported by the Chinese. Late in the year 1884, the reform group, aided by some Japa-

[2] Isabella Bird Bishop, *Korea and Her Neighbors* (New York: Fleming R. Revell & Co., 1897), p. 446.

[3] *The Korea Review,* Homer B. Hulbert, ed. (Seoul: Methodist Publishing House, January 1904), IV (No. 1), 16-20.

nese in Seoul, arose in revolt. The American minister to
Korea, Lucius H. Foote, described the event in a report to
the State Department on December 17, 1884.

We are in the midst of great excitement and, I may say, danger.
It seems that the entire movement is an attempted revolution,
concocted by a few ill advised young men. . . . Ostensibly dis-
satisfied with the non-progressive spirit manifested by the leading officials, they determined to seize the Government, obtain
control of the person of the King, and to administer public
affairs for their own purposes. . . .[4]

The revolt was doomed from the start, since the Chinese,
now showing renewed interest in their ancient dependency, maintained a troop near Seoul to support the status
quo. However, before the revolt had ended, Japan dispatched her troops to the peninsula with the avowed aim
of protecting her nationals and concessions. China responded by sending additional reinforcements and a war
between the two powers seemed unavoidable. But since
neither party was prepared to fight, a conference was held
at Tientsin in April 1885, in which both sides agreed to
withdraw their troops from Korea and further agreed not
to send new troops to the scene without first notifying the
other power.

The Tientsin compact postponed the Chinese-Japanese
conflict a decade. In 1894, new agitation in the peninsula
brought both parties to the scene. In April of that year a
Korean society called the Tonghaks rose up in revolt in
the southern provinces and began a march on Seoul. The
fearful Korean ruler appealed once more to China. Peiping
dispatched 5500 troops and notified the Japanese, in accordance with their agreement. The Japanese reaction was

---

[4] *Korean-American Relations,* Documents Pertaining to the Far Eastern
Diplomacy of the United States, The Initial Period 1883–1886 (Berkeley
and Los Angeles: Univ. of Calif. Press, 1951), I, 97.

to dispatch 8000 of their own troops to the peninsula. The Tonghak uprising, meanwhile, subsided, leaving China and Japan facing each other in the field.

On this occasion the conflict, known in history as the Sino-Japanese war, began on July 25, 1894. The Tokyo government's formal declaration of war was announced on August 1, 1894, and in it Japan complained of China's habit "to designate Korea as her dependency, and openly and secretly to interfere with her domestic affairs." [5]

The Sino-Japanese war lasted but eight months, during which time Japan's modernized army swept the battlefields, seizing Korea and south Manchuria's Liaotung peninsula, while the Japanese navy humiliated China on the seas. Japan's victory was wholly unexpected; the outside world had assumed that China, with her vast population, would quickly bring the islanders to their knees. The war was formally ended on April 12, 1895, by the Treaty of Shimonoseki, in which China was forced to recognize the full and complete independence of Korea, ending a thousand-year relationship. Japan, by this treaty, also obtained possession of Formosa and other rights.

Throughout this period Japan's proclaimed aims had been to aid Korea reform itself and to guarantee Korean independence. But within a few short months of their victory, Japanese heavy-handed efforts to reform the country led to the murder, on October 8, 1895, of the Korean Queen Min, an active foe of Japanese influence. Now a popular reaction against Japan set in. On February 11, 1896, the indecisive Korean king, who had been a virtual prisoner of the Japanese in his palace, managed to elude his guards and flee with his son, the crown prince, to the Russian legation in Seoul, where he received diplomatic

---

[5] *Source Materials on Korean Politics and Ideologies,* Donald G. Tewksbury, ed. (New York: Institute of Pacific Relations, 1950), pp. 7-8.

protection. The startled Japanese found themselves facing an uncooperative Korean populace and, far worse, a new claimant for Korean influence—Tsarist Russia.

The arrival of the Russians upon the scene had followed a long period in which Moscow had expanded its influence eastward across Siberia. As early as 1741, this Russian eastward movement created friction with China along the Amur river. A hundred years later the Russian governor of eastern Siberia developed the idea of establishing a naval base in Pacific waters. In 1858, by the Treaty of Aigun, China ceded certain territories in northern Manchuria to Russia. It was this concession which led, in 1860, to the founding of the port of Vladivostok. According to Historian Bernard Pares, the plan of Tsarist Russia during this period was nothing less than the establishment of Russian rule over all of Asia, including the expulsion of the British from India.[6] So it became only a matter of time before Russia's expanding empire collided, in Korea and Manchuria, with that of Japan.

Bitter feelings between the two nations developed as a result of Japan's victory over China. During the fighting Japan seized the important Liaotung peninsula, which Russia also coveted. The Russian minister of war, General Alexie N. Kuropatkin, commenting later on this, wrote: ". . . we [Russia], in conjunction with the other Powers, compelled Japan [in 1895] to abandon Port Arthur and the Kuan-tung Peninsula, which she had conquered. This, the first of the actions of Russia to excite Japan's hostility, was also by far the most decisive."[7] What compelled Japan was the veiled threat of force in the form of the naval

[6] Pares, *A History of Russia* (New York: Alfred A. Knopf, 1926), p. 428.
[7] Alexie N. Kuropatkin, *The Russian Army and the Japanese War*, A. B. Lindsay, trans. (New York: E. P. Dutton & Co., 1909), p. 151.

squadrons of Russia, France, and Germany, which were cruising Far Eastern waters.

This incident was followed by the flight of the Korean ruler to the Russian legation, placing the Japanese completely on the defensive. Wrote Hulbert:

All their efforts to consolidate their power in Korea, and to secure there some fruit of the victory in the war just finished, had been worse than thrown away. The King had cast himself into the arms of Russia, and the whole Korean people were worked up [after the queen's slaying] to a white heat against Japan, comparable only with the feelings elicited by the invasion of 1592. . . .[8]

The Japanese tried to save the situation, sending emissaries to the king with pleas that he return to the palace. He refused them. Not until a year later did he leave the Russians' protection, and in that time Japanese influence dwindled while Russian influence grew. Training of the Korean army was taken out of Japanese hands and given to the Russians. Military instructors and other advisers arrived from Moscow. It was clear that the Russians had embarked upon an active and highly successful program in Korea.

Russian diplomats also were increasingly active in China. In May 1896, a secret treaty of alliance aimed at Japan was signed between Russia and China, in which the Chinese consented to the construction of a railway across Manchuria in the direction of Vladivostok. On September 8, 1896, a contract for the construction was completed. On March 27, 1898, the Russians also obtained China's signature for a lease to Russia for twenty-five years of the two

[8] Homer B. Hulbert, *The Passing of Korea* (New York: Doubleday, Page & Co., 1906), p. 149.

ports of Talienwan (Dairen) and Port Arthur at the base of the Liaotung peninsula.[9]

This latter development was particularly obnoxious to the Japanese, who had been forced out of the peninsula after their Chinese victory. The Russians, in an effort to calm the angry Tokyo government, hastened to sign an agreement in which Japan and Russia recognized the sovereignty and "entire independence of Korea," but which also recognized Japan's predominant economic influence there. Despite this agreement, the intense Russo-Japanese rivalry continued.

Japan now was awakened to the fact she would have to defeat the Russians in Korea and Manchuria before her own ambitions could be fulfilled. To prepare herself, at the turn of the century Japan began rebuilding her military strength. At the same time Japanese diplomats sought to obtain outside assistance in the event of a new war. In January 1902, these latter efforts were rewarded by an important alliance with Great Britain, an old competitor of Russia. The Japanese also successfully wooed their giant neighbor across the Pacific. The United States, President Theodore Roosevelt assured the Tokyo government, would be benevolent toward Japan in the event of war.[10]

In the summer of 1903 the Japanese brought matters to a head by formally proposing to Russia that the question of Korea and Manchuria be reopened. The Russians agreed and a conference was quickly convened in St. Petersburg (Leningrad). During the next seven months, the talks dragged on fruitlessly as each side offered proposals and counterproposals, one of which was a Russian suggestion that a neutral zone be created along the northern border

[9] *Second Report on Progress in Manchuria to 1930* (Dairen: The South Manchuria Railway, April 1931), pp. 232-245.

[10] Tyler Dennett, *Roosevelt and the Russo-Japanese War* (New York: Doubleday, Page & Co., 1925), p. 27.

between Korean and Russian territory. The Japanese grew impatient while the confident Russians continued to procrastinate. In Tokyo a war party, which had been urging decisive action, finally won over the government. On February 3, 1904, the Japanese delegate at the St. Petersburg negotiations broke off the discussions and departed. Three days later Japan launched her attack on Russian Far Eastern forces. In her declaration of war proclaimed on February 10, Japan charged the Russians had been threatening the independence of Korea.

The outcome of the Russo-Japanese war of 1904–05 was even more astounding than that of the Sino-Japanese war of the previous decade. The Russian armies, handicapped at having to defend an unpopulated frontier territory thousands of miles from the center of Russia's population and industry, were soundly defeated by the Japanese, who overwhelmed Port Arthur and Dairen in a series of bloody assaults. In May 1905, the final blow fell in Tsushima Bay. There the Japanese destroyed the Russian Baltic fleet, which had sailed halfway around the world in an effort to save the situation.

Japan's tremendous victory over Russia on land and sea signaled the rise of a new world power. In Russia it stirred the revolutionary fervor of 1905, the prelude to 1917. In Korea it signaled that country's death knell.

The Japanese and Russians accepted President Roosevelt's offer of his "good offices" to end the war and, on September 5, 1905, they met at Portsmouth, New Hampshire, to sign a peace treaty. Roosevelt's role in this affair, for which he received a Nobel peace prize, has often been cited by Koreans as a betrayal of the United States-Korea Treaty of 1882. Roosevelt clearly did ignore Korean interests in his concern over the attempts of the European powers to

carve out spheres of influence in China. He particularly
felt that Tsarist Russia was guilty of an expansionist policy
in Asia; he feared the Russians, if they could, would "organize northern China against us and rule us absolutely
out of all the ground she can control...." [11] In hopes of im-
plementing the United States "Open Door" policy in Asia,
Roosevelt had given strong support to Japan in opposing
Russia's activities, and he approved Japan's program for
Korea. [12]

But following Japan's amazing military victories over
Russia, Roosevelt's attitude became somewhat less friendly.
Not having anticipated Japan's sudden rise, he felt it necessary to issue a veiled warning to the Japanese minister in
Washington that if Japan now proceeded into a career of
insolence and aggression, it would be "unpleasant" for the
island empire. [13] However, there was another matter for
Roosevelt to consider, the Philippine Islands, which had
been acquired by the United States only a few years before
in the war with Spain. On July 29, 1905, Roosevelt's Secretary of War, William Howard Taft, visited Tokyo and
signed a secret agreement with Japan, that, in return for
Japan's disavowals of aggressive designs on the Philippines,
the United States would agree to establishment of Japan's
suzerainty over Korea.

The Portsmouth peace delegates were assembling when
two Koreans—Pastor Pyung Koo Yoon and a patriot destined for much future fame, Syngman Rhee—sought an
audience with Roosevelt. [14] The President received them

[11] *The Letters of Theodore Roosevelt,* The Square Deal, 1903–1905
(Cambridge: Harvard University Press, 1951), IV, 831.

[12] *Ibid.,* II, 1394.

[13] *Ibid.,* IV, 830.

[14] An authoritative account of Rhee's early activities on behalf of Korea
is given in Robert T. Oliver's *Syngman Rhee, The Man Behind the Myth*
(New York: Dodd Mead & Co., 1954).

cordially, looked at their petition on behalf of Korea, and then suggested they forward it through official channels. This was a convenient way of sidetracking the matter, which had already been settled in Japan's favor. Another appeal, from the Korean emperor (he took the title in 1896 for reasons of prestige), was also rejected by Roosevelt as impractical. In justifying his position, Roosevelt argued that the Koreans "couldn't strike one blow in their own defense" and that they had shown "utter inability" to stand by themselves.[15]

In the months and years which followed the Portsmouth peace, Japan proceeded to assume full control of Korea's economic, political, and social life. On August 22, 1910, Japan formally annexed Korea and during the next three decades ruled the peninsula, renamed Chosen, as a colony and integral part of their empire. Only Japan's calamitous defeat in World War II ended the Koreans' servitude.

We have seen how Korea's destiny, after 1876, was intertwined with the northeast Asia power conflict between Japan, China, and Russia. As a result of its military victories, Japan emerged the strongest power in Asia and the world accepted the absorption of Korea. But although Korea's international status had ended, the Koreans themselves could not so easily forget their ancient kingdom, and many Korean patriots, in and out of Korea, kept alive the dream of independence.

Among them were two outstanding personalities—Rhee, and the famed Kim Koo, who proceeded to organize an underground movement to resist Japanese rule. Both, however, embarked on an almost forty-year exile, Rhee spending much of his time in the United States where he pleaded his country's cause, and Kim Koo living in China. During

15 *The Letters of Theodore Roosevelt*, IV, 1112 and 1116.

the years after Portsmouth, Rhee studied at several American universities, receiving his doctorate from the hands of Woodrow Wilson, president of Princeton University.

After Wilson attained the Presidency of the United States and proclaimed his famous fourteen points in January 1918, near the end of World War I, Rhee was inspired to take vigorous steps to attain his country's freedom. He conceived the idea of a nationwide, nonviolent Korean movement to demonstrate to the world that, despite thirteen years of Japanese rule, Korea yearned for independence and self-determination. Early in 1919, after winning Kim Koo's agreement to his plan, Rhee dispatched a message to the Korean underground:

"President Wilson of the United States has proclaimed a fourteen point program of world peace. One of these points is the self-determination of peoples. You must make the most of this situation. Your voice must be heard. President Wilson will certainly help you." [16]

After highly secret preparations, on March 1, 1919, the Koreans began nationwide nonviolent demonstrations. While thousands marched in protest through the streets of Seoul and other cities, to the dismay of the Japanese, thirty-three Korean leaders met and signed a Korean Declaration of Independence: "We herewith proclaim the independence of Korea and the liberty of the Korean people. . . ." The Japanese, overcoming their initial surprise, reacted with the sword. Thousands of the demonstrators were killed and hundreds of others jailed and tortured.

The Koreans had voiced their desire for independence, but the world showed only passing interest in the "colonial uprising," and within a short time the Japanese had complete control of the situation. It was a bitter lesson for

---

[16] Louise Yim, *My Forty Year Fight for Korea* (New York: A. A. Wyn 1951), p. 30. Miss Yim was a member of the Korean underground.

the Koreans. The Great Powers meeting at Versailles found it expedient to ignore them and their appeals, since Japan was a victor in World War I. As for Wilson, upon whom so much faith was placed, he soon was without power himself, foundering in the discord of a United States Senate which rejected his League of Nations.

Although brutally suppressed, the demonstrations of March 1919 worried the Japanese sufficiently so that they undertook a review of their Korean policies. They subsequently withdrew the military governor and established a more civilian form of authority in Seoul.[17] In addition to this reform, Tokyo also proclaimed that henceforth Korea and Japan were integral parts of the same empire and that Koreans would be treated as Japanese, the "loyal subjects of the same sovereign." To symbolize this, arrangements were consummated for the marriage of a Korean prince to a Japanese princess.

Having suffered an almost mortal blow, the Korean independence movement was driven entirely into exile. In Shanghai, Rhee and Kim Koo defiantly proceeded to organize a Korean Provisional Government, with Rhee named as first President. Another center of resistance formed around the thousands of refugee Koreans who had fled to the Manchurian-Siberian provinces bordering Korea. The Japanese admitted that these latter Koreans had allied themselves "with Russian Bolsheviki" and were conducting guerrilla raids in the area.[18]

In the bleak 1920's and 1930's, the independence movement developed three centers: (1) the "Russian" Koreans, located in the Soviet maritime provinces; (2) the "Chinese" Koreans, who made up the bulk of the Korean Provisional

---

[17] *Annual Report on Reforms and Progress in Chosen (1918–21)* Compiled by Governor-General of Chosen, Keijo (Seoul), December 1921, p. 6.
[18] *Ibid.*, p. 19.

Government and a few army divisions supported by Chiang Kai-shek's Nationalist government; and (3) the "American" Koreans, located in Hawaii and Washington. Rhee was associated with the Chinese and American groups. However, without power of any sort, the exiles were in constant conflict with each other in efforts to gain control of the movement. On one occasion, the Communists approached Rhee for support of the Soviet faction but he rejected their advances.

Korea's resurrection as a nation remained a dream until Japan's attack on Pearl Harbor and American involvement in World War II. Now the languishing hopes of the Korean exiles were suddenly revived. By 1943, as the great conflict grew in intensity, it became increasingly clear that Japan and her Axis partners had lost the war. The Koreans in exile waited nervously, impatiently, for the defeat of the Japanese and their country's liberation.

# 2

# 1943
# The Cairo Pledge

I F AMERICANS thought at all of Korea in the event-filled days following the Pearl Harbor attack, it was as an ancient kingdom overrun by the Japanese a half century before, one of the earliest victims of Japan's aggression. That the defeat of Japan would bring freedom to the Koreans as well as the other subjugated peoples of Asia was an acceptable proposition, and from it stemmed the famous reference to Korea in the Cairo Declaration, issued December 1, 1943, which marked the formal re-entrance of the United States on the Korean scene.

At Cairo, President Franklin Roosevelt, Prime Minister Winston Churchill, and Generalissimo Chiang Kai-shek met late in November 1943, and pledged their nations to persevere in the Pacific war until they had won the unconditional surrender of Japan; in addition, they promised: "The aforesaid three great powers, mindful of the enslavement of the people of Korea, are determined that in due course Korea shall become free and independent." [1] This statement became the wheel around which much future Korean history turned. To understand fully how it came about, however, we must go somewhat afield and examine the important events and decisions which brought

[1] State Department, *Selected Documents on American Foreign Policy* (Washington: Government Printing Office, 1951), p. 10.

about the meeting between Roosevelt, Churchill, and Chiang.

Long before the Japanese attack on Pearl Harbor, the military planners of the United States agreed that, as between Germany and Japan, Hitler's regime was the most dangerous enemy. They agreed that, in the event of the United States' involvement in the war, the European theater should be given the first priority. Admiral Harold R. Stark's view, reflecting that of most American military men, was that "If Britain wins decisively against Germany, we would win everywhere; but that if she loses the problem confronting us would be very great; and, while we might not *lose everywhere,* we might, possibly, not *win* anywhere." [2]

Following Japan's attack, a somewhat relieved Churchill and his military chiefs arrived in Washington on December 23, 1941, for consultations with Roosevelt and American military leaders on strategic planning. Of these meetings, General George C. Marshall, the Army chief of staff, reported: "The President and the Prime Minister, with the advice of the Combined [British-American] Chiefs of Staff, made the decision at this first conference that our resources would be concentrated first to defeat Germany, the greater and closer enemy, and then Japan." [3] Marshall was a staunch advocate of the defeat-the-Germans-first strategy, Churchill has recorded.[4]

The implications of this European orientation were tre-

[2] Maurice Matloff and Edwin M. Snell, *Strategic Planning for Coalition Warfare, 1941–42* in *United States Army in World War II* (Washington: Government Printing Office, 1953), p. 25.

[3] *The War Reports of Generals George C. Marshall, H. H. Arnold, and Fleet Admiral Ernest J. King* (Philadelphia: J. B. Lippincott Co., 1947), p. 153.

[4] Winston S. Churchill, *The Grand Alliance* (Boston: Houghton Mifflin Co., 1950), p. 705.

mendously significant as far as the Far East was concerned. The Pacific theater, under General Douglas MacArthur's command, would get secondary priority on supplies and equipment while China, which had been fighting Japan since 1937, was relegated to the bottom of the wartime logistical pipeline. The result was that the resistance of Chiang Kai-shek's Nationalist government appeared in danger of extinction by the fall of 1942, especially since the Japanese completely isolated China by a successful land campaign in Burma the previous spring.

During these dark days, while Washington had nightmares of a Chinese collapse, General Joseph W. Stilwell attempted to get Chungking to reform and reorganize its armies for a difficult Burma campaign. Chiang Kai-shek, however, opposed this strategy after becoming convinced that a United States air offensive—as advocated by his friend, Maj. Gen. Claire Chennault of the famed "Flying Tigers"—was the best approach to the problem of defeating the Japanese.[5] The Chinese leader's views were made known to Roosevelt. The President, as noted by Herbert Feis in *The China Tangle,* acceded to Chiang's pleading:

He engaged the American government to make a much greater effort in the air for and in China—as rapidly as the greater number of planes could be handled there. At the same time, however, he reaffirmed the opinions of the War Department: that air transport and air combat alone would not be enough to strike a vital blow at Japanese forces in China or Japan, and that it was essential to reopen a land route through Burma. . . .[6]

[5] Charles F. Romanus and Riley Sunderland, *Stilwell's Mission to China* in *United States Army in World War II* (Washington: Government Printing Office, 1953), p. 260.

[6] Herbert Feis, *The China Tangle* (Princeton: Princeton University Press, 1953), p. 59.

In pursuit of the latter goal, the Combined Chiefs of Staff, on May 8, 1943, in a London meeting, drew up a program for intensified China-Burma-India activity, including a plan for an assault upon Japanese forces in Burma by combined British-American-Chinese forces.[7] Chiang, however, was still reluctant to commit his forces to a Burma campaign; before he would do so, he asked assurance of British and American naval support, including an amphibious landing against south Burma. It was to obtain Chinese cooperation that Roosevelt, during the summer of 1943, suggested to Chiang that they meet sometime during the autumn, midway between their two capitals, to discuss mutual problems. This meeting finally was consummated at Cairo.

Before the Cairo conference began, Roosevelt had decided to support China as one of the Great Powers in signing the Moscow Declaration at the Moscow meeting of foreign ministers (Oct. 18-30, 1943). Moreover, Roosevelt went to Cairo, Robert Sherwood wrote, determined "that this conference should be a success from the Chinese point of view." [8] As the meeting got underway, Roosevelt "went down the line" in supporting Chiang's position for an amphibious assault to support Burmese operations. Later, however, following the Anglo-American conference with Stalin at Teheran, Churchill succeeded in changing Roosevelt's mind about the large-scale amphibious operations which had been promised the Chinese.[9] Priority on landing equipment was to be given the Normandy invasion.

[7] Romanus and Sunderland, *op. cit.*, p. 332.
[8] Robert E. Sherwood, *Roosevelt and Hopkins: An Intimate History* (New York: Harpers & Brothers, 1948), p. 772.
[9] Churchill, *Closing the Ring* (Boston: Houghton Mifflin Co., 1951), p. 328.

Where does Korea fit into this picture of war strategy? It seems almost like an afterthought and was of relatively minor interest. The President, Churchill, and Chiang agreed to make a public declaration, which was also shown and approved by Stalin at Teheran. This declaration read as follows:

The several military missions have agreed upon future military operations against Japan. The Three Great Allies expressed their resolve to bring unrelenting pressure against their brutal enemies by sea, land and air. This pressure is already rising.

The Three Great Allies are fighting this war to restrain and punish the aggression of Japan. They covet no gain for themselves and have no thought of territorial expansion. It is their purpose that Japan shall be stripped of all the islands in the Pacific which she has seized or occupied since the beginning of the first World War in 1914, and that all the territories Japan has stolen from the Chinese, such as Manchuria, Formosa, and the Pescadores, shall be restored to the Republic of China. Japan will also be expelled from all other territories which she has taken by violence and greed. The aforesaid three great powers, mindful of the enslavement of the people of Korea, are determined that in due course Korea shall become free and independent.

With these objects in view, the three Allies, in harmony with those of the United Nations at war with Japan, will continue to persevere in the serious and prolonged operations necessary to procure the unconditional surrender of Japan.[10]

That particularly unfortunate phrase "in due course" included in the sentence on Korea evoked understandable misgivings among the Korean exiles. Kim Koo in Chungking denounced the phrase as "absurd" and he demanded his country be given freedom "the moment the Japanese

[10] State Department, Selected Documents. . . . p. 10.

collapse." [11] The phrase and the thinking behind it were unquestionably Roosevelt's. The President held the view that the liberated colonial peoples of Asia should come under the tutelage of the great powers and be educated in the democratic tradition.

I like to think [Roosevelt said on November 15, 1942] that the history of the Philippines in the last forty-four years provides in a very real sense a pattern for the future of other small nations and peoples of the world. It is a pattern of what men of good will look forward to in the future—a pattern of a global civilization which recognizes no limitations of religion or of creed or of race.

[But, Roosevelt continued], we must remember that such a pattern is based on two important factors. The first is that there be a period of preparation through the dissemination of education and the recognition and fulfillment of physical and social and economic needs. The second is that there be a period of training for ultimate independent sovereignty, through the practice of more and more self-government, beginning with local government and passing on through the various steps to complete statehood. [12]

Pursuing this idea in meetings with British Foreign Secretary Anthony Eden on March 27, 1943, Roosevelt suggested, Cordell Hull recorded: ". . . that a trusteeship be set up for Indo-China, that Manchuria and Formosa be returned to China and that Korea might be placed under an international trusteeship, with China, the United States, and one or two other countries participating." [13] Later that year, at one of his first meetings at Teheran

11 *Facts on File Yearbook, 1943* (New York: Persons' Index Facts on File, Inc.,) III, 388.

12 *The Public Papers and Addresses of Franklin D. Roosevelt*, the 1942 Volume, Samuel Rosenman, ed. (New York: Harpers & Bros., 1942), pp. 473-476.

13 Cordell Hull, *The Memoirs of. . . .* (2 vols., New York: The Macmillan Company, 1948), II, 1596.

with Stalin, on November 28, 1943, Roosevelt again "referred to one of his favorite topics, which was the education of the peoples of the Far Eastern colonial areas, such as Indo-China, Burma, Malaya and the East Indies, in the arts of self-government; he pointed with pride to the American record in helping the peoples of the Philippines to prepare themselves for independence . . ." [14] One wonders if Roosevelt was aware, in the case of Korea, of the centuries-long rivalries of the great powers to control the peninsula. Probably he was, but in 1943, at the height of Russo-American amity, the President's vision was that a new and peaceful world, led by men of good will, would emerge from the holocaust.

If the Cairo meeting can be said to be a milestone for the Koreans, the meeting of the Anglo-American leaders with Stalin at Teheran also held fateful portends, for it was there that the Soviet ruler casually announced that once Germany had collapsed, Russia would join in the war against Japan. [15]

The Americans were delighted by Stalin's promise. It was confirmation of similar assurances he had given Secretary Hull at the foreign ministers' conference in Moscow a few weeks before, and it was fulfillment of a long-sought American goal to get Soviet cooperation in the Pacific war. Indeed, within weeks after the Pearl Harbor attack one aspect of the U.S. Air Forces' planning had to do with American air operations in Soviet Siberia. The Americans, in the face of declared Soviet neutrality in the Far East, sought to open negotiations by asking the Russians for information on air facilities in Siberia to facilitate deliveries of lend-lease planes. [16] But these efforts proved in

---

[14] Sherwood, *op. cit.*, p. 777.
[15] Churchill, *Closing the Ring*, p. 349.
[16] Matloff and Snell, *op. cit.*, pp. 142-146.

vain; the Russians were determined not to stir up the Japanese in Manchuria at a moment when they were meeting the onslaught of Hitler's armies in the West.

In view of this, in March 1942, the United States military establishment recommended to President Roosevelt that he "initiate steps on the political level looking toward a more complete military collaboration between the United States and the U.S.S.R." [17] It was not until the Teheran conference and Stalin's announcement that these American efforts—which stretched over a period of almost two years—bore fruit.

Why the Americans wanted the Russians in the Far East war is clear even to the amateur strategist: An attack on three fronts (Chinese, Russian, and American) would shorten the war by many months. The Joint Chiefs of Staff estimated it would take eighteen months after the defeat of Germany, and countless casualties, to defeat Japan. Therefore, the cooperation of the Soviet armies was felt to be essential.[18] In retrospect, this was an overestimation of Japanese power, but it seemed sound at the time and there were few voices, if any, raised against the concept of bringing the Soviet Union into the war.

Upon his return from Cairo and Teheran, Roosevelt summed up for the Pacific War Council, an advisory group, the main points on which agreement had been reached with Stalin and Chiang relating to the defeat of Japan and the postwar settlement in the Pacific. Besides restoring to China and Russia the many territories acquired from them by Japan since 1895, the leaders of the Great Powers agreed that Korea was to be under a lengthy tutelage.

[17] *Ibid.*
[18] William D. Leahy, *I Was There* (New York: McGraw-Hill Book Co., 1950), p. 259.

Thirteen months passed between the Cairo-Potsdam conference and the Great Power meeting at Yalta, where the final agreement was signed containing the political conditions Stalin demanded for Soviet participation in the Pacific War.

In preparing for the Crimea conference, the State Department drew up a number of briefing papers for the President, including one on Korea's postwar status which pointed out that the military occupation of Korea by any single power might have serious political repercussions. It was the Department's view that there should be "Allied representation in the army of occupation and in military government in Korea and that such military government should be organized on the principle of centralized administration with all of Korea administered as a single unit and not as separate zones." [19] As for the post-occupation period, the Department supported Roosevelt's concept that some form of international trusteeship be established "until such time as the Koreans are able to govern themselves." [20] The Department added that the position of the Soviet Union in the Far East was such that "it would seem advisable to have Soviet representation on an interim international administration regardless of whether or not the Soviet Union enters the war in the Pacific." [21]

Prior to Roosevelt's departure for Yalta, the JCS re-emphasized its desire for Soviet participation in the war by sending advice to the President that: "Russia's entry at as early a date as possible consistent with her ability to engage in offensive operations is necessary to provide maximum assistance to our Pacific operations. The U.S. will

[19] State Department, *The Conferences at Malta and Yalta: 1945* (Washington: Government Printing Office, 1955), p. 358.
[20] *Ibid.*, p. 359.
[21] *Ibid.*, p. 361.

provide maximum support possible without interfering with our main effort against Japan." [22]

With this advice in mind, the President, after his talks with the Soviet premier, signed the controversial Yalta document. Nowhere in this document, signed also by Churchill and Stalin, was Korea mentioned. It stated:

The leaders of the three Great Powers—the Soviet Union, the United States of America and Great Britain—have agreed that in two or three months after Germany has surrendered and the war in Europe was terminated the Soviet Union shall enter into the war against Japan on the side of the Allies on condition that:

1. The status quo in Outer-Mongolia (The Mongolian People's Republic) shall be preserved;

2. The former rights of Russia violated by the treacherous attack of Japan in 1904 shall be restored, viz:

a. the southern part of Sakhalin as well as the islands adjacent to it shall be returned to the Soviet Union.

b. the commercial port of Dairen shall be internationalized, the preeminent interests of the Soviet Union in this port being safeguarded and the lease of Port Arthur as a naval base of the U.S.S.R. restored.

c. the Chinese-Eastern Railroad and the South-Manchurian Railroad which provides an outlet to Dairen shall be jointly operated by the establishment of a joint Soviet-Chinese Company, it being understood that the preeminent interests of the Soviet Union shall be safeguarded and that China shall retain full sovereignty in Manchuria.

3. The Kuril islands shall be handed over to the Soviet Union.

It is understood that the agreement concerning Outer Mongolia and the ports and railroads referred to above will require concurrence of Generalissimo Chiang Kai-shek. The President

[22] *Ibid.*, p. 396. Edward R. Stettinius, *Roosevelt and the Russians, The Yalta Conference* (New York: Doubleday & Co., 1949), pp. 90-91.

will take measures in order to obtain this concurrence on advice from Marshal Stalin.

For its part the Soviet Union expresses its readiness to conclude with the National Government of China a pact of friendship and alliance between the U.S.S.R. and China in order to render assistance to China with its armed forces for the purpose of liberating China from the Japanese yoke.[23]

As for Korea, in a meeting with Stalin on February 8, 1945, the President brought up the subject. He said he had in mind a trusteeship composed of a Soviet, an American, and a Chinese representative. He said the only true experience the United States had in this matter was in the Philippines, where it had taken about fifty years for the people to be prepared for self-government. He felt that in the case of Korea, the period might be from twenty to thirty years.[24]

Stalin commented that the shorter the better and inquired whether any foreign troops would be stationed in Korea. The President replied in the negative and Stalin expressed his approval of this. Roosevelt also spoke of his feeling that it didn't seem necessary to invite the British to participate in the trusteeship, but that they might be offended if left out. Stalin agreed they would be offended, adding that the Prime Minister might "kill us." [25]

In the six months between the Yalta conference and Japan's surrender on August 14, 1945, great and calamitous events crowded the international scene. In April Roosevelt, the great wartime leader, died; in May Germany surrendered; in July the Allies met once more at

[23] State Department, *United States Relations With China* (Washington: Government Printing Office, 1949), pp. 113-114.
[24] State Department, *The Conferences at Malta and Yalta: 1945*, p. 770.
[25] *Ibid.*

Potsdam; and in August the atom bomb was dropped on Japan.

The new President, Harry S. Truman, was at the Potsdam meeting with Churchill and Stalin to discuss postwar European problems and Far East strategy, when news of the success of the nuclear experiments in the Nevada desert reached him on July 16. Mr. Truman remarked later that the United States had labored "to construct a weapon of such overpowering force that the enemy could be forced to yield swiftly once we could resort to it." [26] Data on the new weapon was brought to Potsdam on July 17 by Secretary of War Henry Stimson. But although the bomb was an overwhelming success, the President, after a conference with his military advisers, decided that, because of the weapon's unknown effects when used against an enemy, the Allies should go ahead with existing military plans. There was no serious thought given to opposing the Russians' planned entry into the war, although Churchill has recorded that "the President and I no longer felt that we needed his [Stalin's] aid to conquer Japan." [27]

The Joint Chiefs of Staff proceeded to hold military talks with the Russians to coordinate strategy. The Russians showed particular interest in any American plans to undertake operations in Korea or the Kuriles. General Marshall told them that there were no American plans for amphibious operations against Korea. (However, the Americans had discussed possible landings in Korea and at Dairen if the Japanese gave in before Soviet troops occupied those areas.)

Meanwhile, as the Potsdam conference proceeded, the Anglo-Americans found their Russian ally in a much less

[26] Harry S. Truman, *Year of Decisions*, Memoirs (New York: Doubleday & Co., 1955), 418.

[27] Churchill, *Triumph and Tragedy* (Boston: Houghton Mifflin Co., 1953), p. 640.

conciliatory mood than he had been at Yalta. In the intervening months between Yalta and Potsdam, numerous little conflicts had arisen. Now, at the Potsdam conference
table, arguments arose about the postwar settlements in
Europe, especially the Polish border question, German
reparations, and the situation in Soviet-controlled Ruma-
nia and Bulgaria. The Russians, flushed with victory and
straddling a prostrate Germany, gave the first indications
of a desire for much more than the spoils of war.

During a meeting on July 22 the Russians brought up
the question of colonies and trusteeships. They indicated
a wish to have a voice in the disposition of Italy's African
colonies, and they also proposed redistribution of the territories that had been under the League of Nations. As
for Korea, they requested an exchange of views on trusteeship for the peninsula. The Anglo-American Allies, a little
perturbed by the Russians' proposals, agreed to refer these
matters to the foreign ministers.

While the three heads of State argued about postwar
settlements, the JCS was proceeding with preparations
(having received the President's approval) for dropping
the atom bomb on Japan. Beforehand, however, an effort
was made to give the Japanese an opportunity to surrender. An Allied ultimatum was broadcast to the Japanese
from Potsdam, calling on them to surrender uncondition-
ally. The ultimatum reaffirmed the Cairo pledge to limit
Japanese sovereignty to "the islands of Honshu, Hok-
kaido, Kyushu, Shikoku, and such minor islands as we
determine." [28]

The Japanese, in a radio response, rejected the Potsdam
ultimatum and the fateful action was set in motion. On
August 6 the first atom bomb was dropped on Hiroshima;

[28] State Department, *Selected Documents,* p. 10.

on August 8 the Russians formally entered the war, announcing their adherence to the Potsdam declaration. Four days later the Soviet armies, reinforced with troops transferred from Europe, began a massive drive into Manchuria and Korea.

# 3

## The Russian-American Occupation
## of Korea and the Moscow Agreement

WHEN DEATH removed the strong hand of Roosevelt from the nation's helm, many affairs suffered and particularly American foreign policy. In the crucial interim before the new President could assert himself—a period lasting perhaps nine months—foreign policy ran of its own momentum. The State Department struggled to come into its own again, but it had been weakened in policy functions by the almost complete subordination to Roosevelt of its secretaries, Hull and Edward R. Stettinius. The secretaries had played but a minor role in many of the President's great wartime decisions and, specifically, they had not been a factor in the Far Eastern agreement.[1]

But, as we noted earlier, the Department was aware of Roosevelt's plans for a Korean trusteeship. With these in mind, it sought, in the spring of 1945, to encourage the exiled Koreans in the United States to form a coalition so as to have a nucleus to work with on the many problems expected to arise under trusteeship. However, one prominent exile, Rhee, refused to join, insisting, in many speeches, articles, and press conferences, that the best course for the American government would be to recognize the Korean Provisional Government in Chungking, with which he had been long associated. Rhee had become fearful of Soviet postwar efforts to control Korea and

[1] Stettinius, *op. cit.*, p. 95; Hull, *op. cit.*, p. 1584.

he became especially alarmed, in May 1945, when he
heard rumors that a secret agreement had been made at
Yalta to turn Korea over to the Soviets.[2] Having scarcely
forgotten the events of 1904–05, when Korea "was sold
down the river," Rhee called a press conference and publicly charged that such a secret deal had been made.

In response, the Department, on June 8, 1945, denied
any such secret agreement and reaffirmed the United
States' intention to fulfill its commitment made under the
Cairo Declaration. Acting Secretary of State Joseph C.
Grew explained that the United States could not recognize the Korean Provisional Government because it had
"never exercised administrative authority over any part of
Korea, nor can it be regarded as representative of the
Korean people of today. Due to geographical and other
factors its following even among exiled Koreans is inevita-
bly limited." [3] Grew assured the Koreans that the United
States government had "spent a great deal of time in study-
ing the problem relating to Korea and . . . talked at length
with various individuals interested in the welfare of Korea
and the Koreans. . . ." [4] These studies, of course, related
primarily to the concept of tutelage for the Korean people, and concrete decisions and agreements were held in
abeyance pending the end of the war.

V-J Day came, but with such unexpected suddenness
that the United States government was caught unprepared.
The first report of an impending Japanese surrender was
received on August 10, only four days after the atom bomb

[2] Oliver, *op. cit.*, p. 200.
[3] *Documents on American Foreign Relations, 1944–1945* (Norwood, Mass.:
World Peace Foundation, 1947), VII, 230-231.
[4] *Documents on American Foreign Relations, 1944–1945, op. cit.*, pp.
230-231.

was dropped on Hiroshima. Now United States planning had to be switched abruptly from invasion strategy to that of occupation and disarmament of the enemy.

Into the feverish atmosphere of Washington following Japan's surrender offer came several troubled reports from President Truman's representative on reparations in Moscow, Edwin W. Pauley, and Averell Harriman, the Ambassador to Russia. Both men urged, in view of growing Russian intransigence on several issues, that the United States now proceed with landings in Korea and Manchuria to accept the surrender of Japanese troops. "I cannot see," Harriman reported, "that we are under any obligation to the Soviets to respect any zone of Soviet military operation." [5]

These recommendations, and early State planning on the Korean occupation, were followed up as the Army authorities proceeded to draw up a directive to the Japanese forces in the field to lay down their arms and, specifically, to whom they were to surrender. The nightmarish 38th parallel division grew out of this directive. In China, Formosa, and Indo-China north of the 16th parallel, the Japanese were to surrender to Chiang Kai-shek. In Manchuria, and Korea north of the 38th parallel, and on Karfuto, they would surrender to the Russians. Of Korea, Truman recalled:

I was told that Secretary [of State James F.] Byrnes had suggested that American forces receive the surrender as far north as practicable. The Army authorities, however, were faced with the insurmountable obstacles of both distance and lack of manpower. Even the 38th parallel was too far for any American troops to reach if the Russians had chosen to disagree. . . . By drawing it along the 38th parallel, our military as-

[5] Truman, *Year of Decisions*, pp. 433-434.

sured us of the opportunity to receive the surrender in Korea's ancient capital city, Seoul. . . .[6]

There was no thought, Truman said, of a permanent division of Korea.

General Order No. 1, which embodied the surrender directive, was reviewed and approved by the State-War-Navy Coordinating Committee on August 11 and 12, the Joint Chiefs of Staff on August 14, and finally by the President.[7] On August 15 it was dispatched to General MacArthur in Manila, and, at the same time, communicated to the Russians, British, and Chinese. Stalin, in accordance with the order, directed his forces to halt in Korea in the vicinity of the parallel.

Now preparations for the American occupation began. MacArthur looked to Okinawa, six hundred miles from Korea, for an American occupation force, and decided upon Lt. Gen. John R. Hodge's XXIV Corps, which had fought across the Pacific. MacArthur's only political directive from Washington at this time was reference to the Cairo Declaration and he quoted this in his General Order to the people of Korea in asking their aid and compliance in enforcing the Japanese surrender.

General Hodge, a tough, successful combat officer, began to prepare for the new assignment in Korea, but he found himself hampered by little or no practical guidance on such questions as the eventuality of Korean independence, methods of handling various political factions, or the severance of Korea from Japanese influence. Wrote one of his staff officers caustically: "If Washington or GHQ had given much constructive thought to Korean problems, it

[6] *Ibid.*, pp. 444-445.
[7] U.S. Congress, Senate, *The United States and the Korean Problem* Documents 1943–1953 (Washington: Government Printing Office, 1953), pp. 2-3.

had not been reflected in orders issued the Corps commander." [8]

The sad truth was that Korea was the only important area occupied by American troops in the Pacific for which detailed, concrete preparation had not been made by any branch of the United States government.[9] General Hodge, uncomfortably aware that he was about to enter an unknown situation, requested that a State Department representative be attached to his staff before he embarked for Korea. A Class II foreign service officer was dispatched from Washington, but he could add little to the sum total of knowledge on over-all policy toward Korea—since there was only the nebulous plan for trusteeship.

In a further search for practical guidance in meeting immediate problems, Hodge's staff thought it found some in General MacArthur's directive, issued August 29, 1945, relating to the Japanese surrender. This directive declared that the Japanese army headquarters should continue to function to aid in the demobilization of the various armies and also, among other things, that property rights of Japanese nationals would be scrupulously respected. Korea was not mentioned in this directive, but it created the extremely unfortunate attitude in XXIV Corps for retention of Japanese officials in their jobs in Korea.

On September 1 and again on September 5, as the date for the planned embarkation of American troops for Korea neared, leaflets were dropped over Korea from B-29 planes, informing the people of the impending arrival of United States troops and appealing to them to avoid internal disorder. The Japanese army commander radioed the Ameri-

[8] "History of United States Army Forces in Korea (USAFIK)," XXIV Corps Historical Section, n.d., Ch. 1, Pt. I, p. 63 (MSS held by Chief of Military History, Department of Army, Washington).

[9] Carl J. Friedrich & Associates, *American Experiences in Military Government in World War II* (New York: Rinehart & Co., 1948), p. 355.

cans a few days later that the leaflets "had caused considerably favorable results for the maintenance of peace and order." [10]

On September 8, almost a month after the first Russian troops had entered Korea, a convoy of American army transports threaded its way into Inchon harbor and troops began to unload as soon as the ships were anchored. The next day the Japanese surrendered in Seoul.

In mid-afternoon on the 9th [wrote an observer], Lt. General John R. Hodge, Commanding General of the XXIV Corps, and Vice Admiral Thomas C. Kinkaid, the Commander of the United States Seventh Fleet, arrived in Seoul to accept the formal surrender of all Japanese south of 38 degrees north latitude. As they drove up the main street to the capitol building, wild enthusiasm broke loose in the city of the kings.[11]

Immediately following the surrender ceremony, General Hodge held a press conference and announced that the Japanese governor-general, Nobuyuki Abe, and other Japanese officials, would be retained in office temporarily in order to facilitate the administration and orderly taking over of the government. This announcement, as was seen earlier, was in emulation of MacArthur's activities in beginning the occupation of Japan. It was a grievous mistake. The Koreans, who had expected their vanquished overlords to be immediately ousted, were astonished. Their dissatisfaction during the next few days became so great that General Hodge felt it necessary to revise his plan and order the replacement of all Japanese officials as soon as possible. On September 12, Governor Abe was relieved of his duties, but American prestige had suffered.

Several weeks elapsed before it dawned on the excited

[10] "History of USAFIK," op. cit., p. 71.
[11] Korea (Far East Command: Troop Information & Education Section, Hqs, XXIV Corps, 1948), p. 46.

Koreans that there were now two foreign armies in their country and that Korea had in some mysterious way been split in two at the 38th parallel. From Seoul, a *New York Times* correspondent, Richard J. H. Johnston, cabled his office at the close of September 1945:

Today the question on the lips of all thinking Koreans, representing every shade of political opinion, is this: Why has our country been divided? Neither the Russians nor the Americans here can answer that. The Koreans' great fear is of what will be inherited by them when the day comes for the removal of Allied controls. Will the country be torn by political strife resulting from the establishment of two opposing ideologies? [12]

The question was prophetic.

The Americans began, soon after their arrival, to tackle the urgent military matters for which they had primarily come: the disarmament and evacuation to Japan of two hundred thousand Japanese troops in southern Korea, most of whom had fled from the advance of the Russian armies. The accomplishment of this task was given first priority. A second enormous job was the repatriation to Korea from the four corners of Asia of almost two million Koreans, an undertaking which began shortly after the Japanese surrender.

As these projects were being implemented, General Hodge turned his attention to a problem with which he was less prepared to deal—the pent-up emotions of the Koreans who feverishly desired immediate independence for their country and who had formed, to the bewilderment of Hodge's staff, more than seventy political organizations prior to the arrival of U.S. forces.[13]

The most active of these was the Korean People's "Re-

[12] *The New York Times,* September 30, 1945.
[13] *Korea* (Far East Command), p. 48.

public," an organization originally created on the initiative of the Japanese. The Japanese, following Japan's surrender, apparently hoped to create a pro-Japanese atmosphere before their eviction by encouraging a group of prominent Koreans to take part in the formation of a committee of patriots which was to act during the transitional post-surrender period. Leader of the committee was a leftist sympathizer named Woon Hyung Lyuh. The Japanese went so far as to allow Lyuh access to press and radio facilities. In August 1945, Lyuh announced over the Japanese radio network that his organization would be responsible for the maintenance of law and order and the principal functions of government. The Japanese soon found events proceeding against their wishes, as these concessions were interpreted by the Koreans as a sign of weakness. As anti-Japanese agitation swept the peninsula, the army moved to reassert Japan's authority pending the arrival of the Americans.

The taste of power had been enough for the Lyuh group and it refused to bend to the Japanese will. It adopted the title of "Republic," and its popularity soon spread among the provinces of the country. By the time the XXIV Corps arrived, the "Republic" appeared to have a legitimate claim that its voice constituted, as no other group had in forty years, the will of the Korean people. However, when the Lyuh group presented itself to General Hodge as a legitimate government, the American commander looked askance. He had no instructions to deal with a Korean government, especially in view of General MacArthur's proclamation to the people of Korea that: "All powers of Government over the territory of Korea south of 38 degrees north latitude and the people thereof will be for the present exercised under my authority." [14]

[14] U.S. Congress, Senate, *The United States and the Korean Problem*, p. 3.

The Lyuh group continued to insist it was a legitimate government. On October 10, 1945, thereupon, Hodge's military governor, Major General A. V. Arnold, issued a statement to the Korean press that "There is only one Government in Korea south of 38 degrees north latitude. It is the government created in accordance with the proclamations of General MacArthur, the general orders of Lieutenant General Hodge and the Civil Administration orders of the Military Governor. . . ." The statement failed to deter the "Republic."

Lyuh, meanwhile, announced he was leaving that organization to form a new political grouping which he called the Korean People's Party. His departure left the "Republic" in the hands of its more radical members. Their defiance reached a peak after General Hodge formally requested they drop the title "Republic" and assume the conventional role of a political party. The group, at a three-day meeting beginning November 20, 1945, ignored the army commander's request. Therefore, on December 12, Hodge publicly denounced the organization, stating that a continuation of its activities as a government was unlawful and that his occupation forces would take the necessary steps against it. This threat proved effective and the group went into decline.

A second important leftist political organization which troubled the American command was the Korean Communist Party, a small but powerful group which the Americans believed to be controlled by Moscow through the Soviet consulate in Seoul. For some inexplicable reason, the consulate had continued to function even though the Russians had entered the war against Japan; it was still in business when the Americans arrived in Seoul.

Of the rightist, conservative elements, two major parties emerged—the Democratic Party and the Nationalist Party.

These organizations were generally more cooperative in the early stages of the American occupation. The Democratic Party, on September 16, 1945, had held a meeting in Seoul and named three famous Korean expatriates—Dr. Rhee, Dr. Philip Jaisohn,* and Kim Koo—as their leaders. All three men, absent from the country, were associated with the Korean Provisional Government.

On October 16, 1945, Rhee, the most important figure in Korea's recent history, returned to the peninsula after his long exile. His return had not been without some difficulty. From the day of Japan's surrender the old patriot, whose home was in Washington, D.C., tried to obtain American permission to travel to Korea. It is clear that the State Department had doubts as to Rhee's value in bringing order to the excited political scene there. He had been a steady critic of the Department and United States policies, and furthermore he was in his seventieth year and had been away from his homeland for many years. However, on his promise that he would return to Korea in the role of a private citizen and not as a member of the Korean Provisional Government, his trip was approved by both the Department and General Hodge. The American commander, who was extremely handicapped by a lack of personnel who could speak Korean and English, hoped to use Rhee as a political adviser.[15]

To the Korean people the return of Rhee was a legend come to life; he was the symbol of their long struggle for independence and his arrival was the occasion for spontaneous celebrations. Rhee's popularity with the people, now no longer doubted, his long residency in the United States, and his almost perfect command of English stood him in good

* Dr. Jaisohn was one of the participants in the revolt of 1884 who later fled abroad and became a United States citizen.
15 "History of USAFIK," Pt. II, Ch. 1, pp. 33-34.

stead. His popularity was so obvious that all the political parties, including the Communists, sought to gain his support. Rhee, however, initially refused to commit himself, undertaking to organize a "Committee for the Rapid Realization of Korean Independence." But within a few months Rhee had made it clear that he was strongly opposed to the Communists and he took a position at the head of the conservative forces.

Several other important exiles returned in November 1945. Kim Koo, president of the Provisional Government in Chungking, also was flown to the peninsula on the promise he would return as a private citizen. His associate at Chungking, Dr. Kim Kiusic, was a third arrival.

Meanwhile, from the north, rumors circulated to Seoul about the arrival from Manchuria of a man called Kim Il Sung, reportedly a guerrilla leader who had fought with the Communists in Manchuria against the Japanese. Welcomed by the Soviet authorities, Kim Il Sung immediately began to organize the nucleus of a North Korean government.

For the Americans, the splintered political situation in Korea was of secondary importance compared with the formidable problem which hovered just north of Seoul—the suspicious Russian army. The Soviets' swift occupation of North Korea having gone unviewed and unpublicized, the Russians appeared to have had little difficulty in establishing rigid, Communist control over the territory. With the arrival of the XXIV Corps on September 8, the Russians agreed to establish tactical liaison at the 38th parallel but, thereafter, the Soviet authorities remained almost entirely unresponsive to General Hodge's overtures.

Within two weeks of the landing of his forces, Hodge became aware of the suspicious atmosphere emanating from the north. One of the first unfriendly acts of the Soviets was to cut off electric power service for an area north of Seoul. Their general deportment was such that Hodge was forced to report to MacArthur that the liaison with the Russians in Korea was anything but satisfactory.

In an effort to bring the Russians around, Hodge twice invited the Soviet commander, Colonel General I. M. Chistiakov, to fly to Seoul to discuss the various pressing economic and political problems which were obviously resulting from the division of the peninsula. Chistiakov's response, in a letter on October 9, 1945, was that he could take no such action as General Hodge suggested because, he said, matters of unification could only be resolved by the governments of the two occupying powers.

This initial exchange of messages set the somber tone of future negotiations between the two military commands, negotiations in which the Americans urged on-the-spot integration of the two zones, while the Russians refused to take any action pending governmental decisions. As the months passed, the situation began to prove disastrous. The 38th parallel boundary had left two-thirds of the Korean people (who totaled about twenty-six million in 1945) and most of the food supply in the south, while most of the country's industry, hydroelectric developments, and resources were in the north. Prices in the southern half, with no chemicals, coal, or goods coming down from the north, began to rise in an inflationary spiral. The American command's efforts to persuade the Soviet command to ship coal and chemicals were futile.

As the situation grew more and more unpromising, the worried Koreans, early in November 1945, organized a meeting in Seoul of all political groups, including the Communists, and issued a joint memorandum demanding they be given the opportunity of organizing Korea as a unified whole. The division of their country, they declared, was "a most serious blunder that is not of our making."[16] By December 1945, this had apparently become evident to all but the Russians. The matter, however, as the Russians in Korea continued to insist, could no longer be settled at the local level.

In Washington, as the reports of Soviet immobility began to flow in, the State-War-Navy Coordinating Committee, on October 20, 1945, laid down American policy on Korea: "The present zonal military occupation of Korea by United States and Soviet Forces should be superseded at the earliest possible date by a trusteeship for Korea."[17] It had become clear to the U.S. government that the Soviets would try to obtain predominant influence in Korea. Warning of this came as early as July 1945, from T. V. Soong, the Chinese foreign minister, who had gone to Moscow to discuss the Yalta agreements. It was Soong's understanding (Harriman reported) that:

The Russians have two Korean divisions trained in Siberia. He believes that these troops will be left in Korea and that there will be Soviet trained political personnel who will also be brought into the country. Under those conditions, he is fearful that even with a four-power trusteeship the Soviets will obtain domination of Korean affairs.[18]

Still the American government felt it had no choice but to proceed with establishment of a trusteeship. On November 10, 1945, President Truman met with Prime Minister Clement Attlee of Britain and Mackenzie King, the Canadian Prime Minister, in Washington, to discuss mutual problems. About Korea, it was agreed that immediate steps

16 *The New York Times,* November 3, 1945.
17 "History of USAFIK," Pt. II, Ch. 4, pp. 57-58.
18 Truman, *Year of Decisions,* pp. 316-317.

should be taken to set up the trusteeship under the direction of the four great powers.[19]

In Korea the American command, including Hodge's newly assigned diplomatic advisers, were strongly opposed to trusteeship. They reported to Washington that the entire trusteeship idea was repugnant to all parties and elements in Korea and that, in view of this unanimous opposition, it might be wise to abandon the trusteeship plan. On November 29, 1945, Secretary Byrnes replied that if, during the impending Moscow Conference, adequate guarantees could be obtained from the Russians for the unification and independence of Korea, it might be possible for the United States to discontinue its support of trusteeship.[20]

The Moscow Conference, planned to iron out the many problems which had arisen between the Allies in Europe and the Far East, began on December 16, 1945. The American delegation, led by Secretary Byrnes, apparently had serious doubts about Soviet cooperation in establishing a truly independent Korea. A trusteeship, with four governments participating, still seemed to be the only way of preventing ultimate domination of Korea by the Soviets. The wishes of the Koreans, the Americans decided, could be ignored for the moment.

Byrnes initiated the discussion on Korea by submitting a paper proposing the establishment of a joint commission to unify the administration of such matters as currency, trade and transportation, telecommunications, electric power distribution, coastal shipping, and so on. He further proposed the creation of a four-power trusteeship, to last for no longer than necessary to allow the Koreans to form an independent, representative government. As to how long such a trusteeship should last, the Americans spoke in terms of five

[19] *Ibid.*, p. 540.
[20] "History of USAFIK," Pt. II, Ch. 4, p. 62.

years, but indicated that the tutelage could be extended by agreement of the four governments. (It will be recalled that only eleven months before, Roosevelt was thinking in terms of a twenty-to-thirty year trusteeship.)

The Russians deliberated on the American proposal for several days. Then, Byrnes reported, Soviet Foreign Minister V. M. Molotov "submitted a Soviet proposal for a Joint Commission on urgent problems of economic unification, the establishment of a provisional government and a four-power trusteeship to last for five years." [21] The American were relieved by the Soviet proposal, which appeared to come toward their viewpoint. They thereupon accepted the Soviet draft, with a few amendments, and it was included in the Moscow declaration. However, the written agreement on Korea contained serious defects which were later to plague the State Department. The full text of the final Moscow agreement bears citation, as follows:

1. With a view to the re-establishment of Korea as an independent state, the creation of conditions for developing the country on democratic principles and the earliest possible liquidation of the disastrous results of the protracted Japanese domination in Korea, there shall be set up a provisional Korean democratic government which shall take all the necessary steps for developing the industry, transport and agriculture of Korea and the national culture of the Korean people.

2. In order to assist the formation of a provisional Korean government and with a view to the preliminary elaboration of the appropriate measures, there shall be established a Joint Commission consisting of representatives of the United States command in southern Korea and the Soviet command in northern Korea. In preparing their proposals the Commission shall consult with the Korean democratic parties and social organizations. The recommendations worked out by the Com-

[21] James F. Byrnes, *Speaking Frankly* (New York: Harpers & Brothers, 1947), pp. 221-222.

mission shall be presented for the consideration of the Governments of the Union of Soviet Socialist Republics, China, the United Kingdom and the United States prior to final decision by the two Governments represented on the Joint Commission.

3. It shall be the task of the Joint Commission, with the participation of the provisional Korean democratic government and of the Korean democratic organizations to work out measures also for helping and assisting (trusteeship) the political, economic and social progress of the Korean people, the development of democratic self-government and the establishment of the national independence of Korea.

The proposals of the Joint Commission shall be submitted, following consultation with the provisional Korean government for the joint consideration of the Governments of the United States, Union of Soviet Socialist Republics, United Kingdom and China for the working out of an agreement concerning a four-power trusteeship of Korea for a period of up to five years.

4. For the consideration of urgent problems affecting both southern and northern Korea and for the elaboration of measures establishing permanent coordination in administrative-economic matters between the United States command in southern Korea and the Soviet command in northern Korea, a conference of the representatives of the United States and Soviet commands in Korea shall be convened within a period of two weeks.[22]

The news of the Moscow agreement reached Korea on the morning of December 29, 1945, just prior to the New Year's celebrations. When the significance of what had been determined for them sank in, the Koreans arose in anger. The conservative forces, led by Kim Koo and Rhee, organized mass demonstrations in the streets of Seoul. The Koreans,

[22] State Department, *Moscow Meeting of Foreign Ministers Dec. 16-26, 1945* (Washington: Government Printing Office, 1946), pp. 14-16.

including initially the Communists,[23] unanimously denounced the Moscow plan, the word "trusteeship" bearing too close a resemblance to the Japanese rule from which they had just emerged. The somewhat shocked American military government sought to interpret the meaning of trusteeship in the most favorable light, but the Koreans refused to listen. The furor was only slightly assuaged by a December 30 broadcast by Secretary Byrnes to the American people on the Moscow conference. Regarding Korea, Byrnes stated that the Joint Commission "may find it possible to dispense with a trusteeship. It is our goal to hasten the day when Korea will become an independent member of the society of nations."[24]

But, as the last hours of 1945, the year of great victory, ticked away, the Koreans remained greatly troubled.

[23] The XXIV Corps later obtained a document, dated January 3, 1946, containing North Korean Communist "Instructions to All Levels and Branches Concerning the Decisions on Korean Problems Made by the Three Power Conference at Moscow." On that day, January 3, the South Korea Communist Party reversed its stand and came out publicly for trusteeship.

[24] State Department, *Moscow Meeting of Foreign Ministers*, p. 6.

# 4

# Failure of the
# Joint Soviet-American Commission

LIAISON BETWEEN Washington and Seoul had been terrible. Hodge and his staff, having received Byrnes' wire that the United States might possibly forego the trusteeship idea at Moscow, were astonished at the decision against immediate Korean independence. They concluded that it was plainly the result of Soviet machinations. As the new year, 1946, began, the Army commander assured Rhee and Kim Koo of his sincere belief that the United States would pursue the goal of early independence for Korea and he asked that they call off the riots and strikes still sweeping the south. The conservative leaders, somewhat assuaged, ordered the strikes ended. However, they continued to agitate against the Soviet Union, accusing the Russians of delaying on Korean independence.

The Soviets, of course, did not remain inactive in this situation. Beginning early in January 1946, the Russian press began attacking the Rhee-Koo conservatives, labeling them as "reactionaries." The Americans subsequently were attacked also for paying heed to the conservative group. Tass, the Soviet news agency, on January 22, 1946, reported from Pyongyang it had been "astonished" at the behavior of the American command. The Americans, Tass said, "had assumed a position of inspiring reactionary demonstrations against the decisions of the Moscow conference of foreign ministers, in which, as is known, the government of the United States participated."[1]

On January 26, the same day General Hodge was branding the Tass statement as "without basis in fact," the chief of the Soviet military mission in Seoul, Colonel General Terenti Shtikov, called a press conference for Korean newspapermen and released a detailed account of the proceedings of the Moscow conference. The purpose of the release, Shtikov stated, was to let the people of Korea know "the true standing of Russia in regards to Korean problems." The substance of the Russian report was that, at Moscow, it had been the United States that had proposed the trusteeship plan for Korea, to last for ten years, whereas the Soviet Union had insisted on limiting the period of trusteeship to "only five years."[2] Thus the Russians donned the mantle of protector of the Korean people.

The Americans in Seoul were greatly embarrassed by the Shtikov press release. Its detailing of the negotiations at Moscow was so impressive that, if true, the ground appeared to have been cut from under the Americans' protestations that the United States stood for immediate Korean independence. Hodge, in a message to Tokyo and Washington following the Shtikov incident, pleaded for information so that he could determine his policies and respond to the Soviet statement.

On January 30, 1946, a State Department report was finally forwarded to the Corps commander, supporting the Russian statement that the United States had been the prime mover behind the trusteeship plan. In explaining why the United States had supported trusteeship, the Department pointed out its goal was to prevent Russian domination of the country. The Moscow agreement was a compromise for-

[1] *The New York Times*, January 23, 1946.
[2] *Ibid.*, January 26, 1946.

mula, the Russians accepting the Anglo-American principle
of trusteeship but with emphasis on Korean "democratic"
parties, social organizations, and provisional government. It
was apparent, the report noted, that the Russians had available various apparatus, in the form of émigré Koreans loyal
to Moscow, to take over the "democratic" provisional government, which would then move to exclude the other powers from Korea. The Soviet attacks on Rhee and Koo, who
were oriented toward the United States and China, probably presaged the position the Russians would take against
"reactionaries" in the impending Soviet-American discussions. They believed their forces would soon win control
over the Korean situation.[3]

The American commander and his staff in Seoul read the
Department's explanation with some amazement. It meant
that the United States had taken a stand on trusteeship completely opposite to that which they had been assuring the
Koreans the American government would take. What could
they say to the Koreans now?

On February 1, 1946, the sadly enlightened General
Hodge dispatched another message to MacArthur, complaining of the lack of guidance. He pointed out that the
Shtikov statement might cause the Koreans to feel that the
United States had sold them out. The statement was clev-
erly worded, he said, to place the United States in a very bad
light. He further pointed out that the Russians were beginning to improve their behavior in the north and through
clever propaganda were claiming the role of savior of thirty
million Korean people. In addition, Communist activity
was on the rise and there was nothing in the attitude of the
Russians to indicate that they had any thought of unifying
Korea while the United States remained there. In his opinion, Hodge said, the country would never be reunited until

[3] "History of USAFIK," Pt. II, Ch. 4, p. 88.

the Russians felt the whole would be communistic. He again pleaded that he be kept informed of American policy, adding that he had the distinct feeling of being let down by the authorities in Washington.[4]

In another message several days later, Hodge offered to accept relief from his post and play the role "of a sacrificial goat" if such action was necessary to save face for the United States with either Russia or Korea.[5]

It was just preceding this strained atmosphere that the Russians and Americans sat down in Seoul in mid-January 1946, in the first of a series of administrative-economic discussions. General Hodge welcomed the Russian delegation, headed by General Shtikov, on January 16, and voiced the hope that the discussions would result in agreement to eliminate the 38th parallel barrier and thus "bring to an end the trials and difficulties of the Korean nation. . . ."[6]

However, it became quite clear in the meetings which followed that a wide gap existed between what the two military commands thought they should accomplish. The Americans wished to discuss immediate, on-the-spot liquidation of the parallel and prompt integration of the two zones. The Russians just wanted to obtain agreements for the delivery of rice and other products from south to north Korea, evacuation of Japanese refugees, and negotiations for delivery of electric power from north to south Korea. The talks dragged on fruitlessly, finally breaking up on February 5, 1946. Little was accomplished toward breaking down the 38th parallel barrier.

On January 28 General Shtikov called upon General Hodge, stating he had received orders from Moscow to make arrangements for the convening of the Joint Soviet-Ameri-

[4] *Ibid.*, pp. 89-91.
[5] *Ibid.*, p. 92.
[6] *Pacific Stars & Stripes*, January 18, 1946.

can Commission to discuss the political unification of Korea. Hodge reported this development to Washington. Among the official Washington directives and guidance he received in preparation for the political discussions was a JCS statement that only those Korean parties, organizations, and individuals considered to be nondemocratic by *both* the United States and Russia should be excluded from participation. The Korean leaders should be representative of the views and aspirations of the Korean people as a whole and also of such composition as to be acceptable to both the United States and the U.S.S.R. No group dominated by totalitarian leftists, such as Communists, or by rightist elements, said the JCS, could be considered as representative of the Korean people and therefore these groups were not acceptable.[7]

In hopes of strengthening his position prior to the opening of the Joint Commission discussions, General Hodge approved the organization, on February 14, 1946, of a *Representative Democratic Council of South Korea.* Hodge sought to obtain a broad political coloration to the council by asking Lyuh and Pak Heun Yung, the latter head of the South Korean Communist Party, to join. The leftists, however, refused to join with the predominant conservatives and the *Council* rapidly became a rightist organization under Rhee as chairman.[8]

Early in March 1946—prior to the convening of the Joint Commission—the State Department issued belated instructions that American policy in Korea be shifted away from the Rhee-Koo forces to progressive leaders. The State Department apparently was relying on information on Korea on Youngjeung Kim, a Korean émigré in Washington, who

[7] "History of USAFIK," p. 145.

[8] George M. McCune, *Korea Today* (Cambridge: Harvard University Press, 1950), p. 50.

publicly stated his opinion that Lyuh was a "liberal and popular leader," while the "old Korean exiles" like Syngman Rhee and Kim Koo were "too old" and lacking in leadership, vision, and statesmanship. Louise Yim, pro-Rhee, stated that Youngjeung Kim had not been in Korea in thirty years and had had nothing to do with politics. Miss Yim was shocked "to learn that some people in the State Department took his word as authoritative."[9] In any event the Department's directive—that support be switched away from Rhee and Kim Koo—arrived too late to change the political picture, although the military government made additional efforts to lure leftists into the *Council.*

Meanwhile, the American delegation to the Joint Commission began holding preparatory conferences in Seoul to discuss the various lines of reasoning and probable arguments the Soviets would make. It was clear to the American delegation, which was headed by General Arnold, that the Soviet Union's long-term strategic aim was to establish complete domination over Korea. United States policy, therefore, would be to insist on some form of territorial guarantee for Korea, since the country, if left alone, could never defend its integrity against Russia. The Russians were expected to push for the early establishment of a "democratic" provisional government and subsequent elimination of the other powers from the peninsula.[10]

On March 20, 1946, the Joint Soviet-American Commission held its first meeting in the Duk Soo palace in Seoul. Both Hodge and Shtikov issued statements at the initial session, which was opened to the press. Shtikov's remarks included the statement that:

In the way of gradual democratization of the whole of the internal life of the Korean people, there stand serious diffi-

---

[9] Yim, *My Forty Year Fight for Korea,* pp. 255-256.
[10] "History of USAFIK," pp. 154-155.

culties, brought about by the furious resistance of reactionary and anti-democratic groups and certain elements whose object is to undermine the work of creating and firmly establishing a democratic system in Korea. . . . The Soviet Union has a keen interest in Korea being a true democratic and independent country, friendly to the Soviet Union, so that in the future it will not become a base for an attack on the Soviet Union. . . .[11]

Following the opening ceremonies, the Commission entered into closed session meetings. Immediately the situation arose which the American delegation had anticipated: the Russians announced that only those Korean parties and organizations which had not opposed the trusteeship principle were eligible for consultation with the Commission in the formation of a government. Since the Korean people almost without exception had opposed the idea of trusteeship, the acceptance of this Russian principle would have meant that only the Communists would be consulted in the formation of a unified government. The Americans rejected this principle at once. In twenty-four fruitless sessions, lasting until May 6, 1946, the issue remained unresolved by the Commission, which adjourned *sine die*.

General Hodge reported to MacArthur the day afterward that he could see no reason for any further negotiations. He stated that at no point in the discussions had there been any indication that the Russians intended to cooperate in the establishment of anything other than a fully Communist-controlled government in Korea.[12]

A few days later General Shtikov called upon General Hodge with the announcement that he had been ordered to stop all work and return north with the entire Soviet delegation. In a final statement on the Soviet position, Shtikov told Hodge:

[11] *Source Materials on Korean Politics and Ideologies,* pp. 77-78.
[12] "History of USAFIK," p. 210.

The main reason why the Soviet delegation insisted on barring certain persons from consultation is that Russia is a close neighbor to Korea and, because of this, is interested in establishing in Korea a provisional democratic government which would be loyal to the Soviet Union. [The Koreans who objected to the Moscow decision and] raised their voices against the Soviet Union slandered the Soviet Union and smeared it with mud. If they seized power in the government, the government would not be loyal to Russia, and its officials would be instrumental in organizing hostile actions on the part of the Korean people against the Soviet Union.[13]

The charge, in view of the comparative sizes of Russia and Korea, was a bit facetious.

On May 15, 1946, Moscow made public its view of the fruitless discussions of the Joint Commission. The newspaper *Izvestia* charged the American delegation had tried to force the Russians to consult with reactionary Korean parties and groups, and had tried to revise the Moscow decision regarding a five-year trusteeship. *Izvestia* said: "The American command not only strove to justify the reactionary parties and organizations against the Moscow decision but also to encourage them in their struggle against the Moscow decisions to mislead the Korean people and to break up the ranks of the genuine democratic parties and organizations."[14]

General Hodge, meanwhile, dispatched a letter to General Chistiakov, the Soviet commander, expressing his willingness to reopen the discussions at any time.

The first major effort to unify Korea had ended in dismal failure. The failure meant that in each zone constructive steps had to be taken at once to improve the unsatisfactory temporary administration. The occupation was suddenly to

[13] *Ibid.,* pp. 212-213.
[14] *The New York Times,* May 16, 1946.

become prolonged. The Soviet regime intensified its policy of communizing North Korea and building a strong native government "loyal" to the U.S.S.R., while in the south the Americans took up a campaign against Communist elements, tried to encourage democratization, and sought to establish an effective Korean administration under the military government.[15]

The American position on Korea was restated on August 30, 1946, by the then Under Secretary of State Dean Acheson. Acheson announced that the United States government was ready to carry out the Moscow decision, including continuation at any time of the work of the Joint Commission. General Hodge, he said, had been instructed to assure the Korean people that the United States would uphold its commitments and would stand by them until these commitments were fully achieved. "We believe," Acheson stated, "in the right of the Korean people to determine for themselves the kind of economy and democratic political organization they require and are opposed to established any minority group in power. We stand for freedom of speech, of assembly, and of the press. Honest criticism is not considered a crime."[16]

But as the first anniversary of the liberation of Korea came and passed, the unhappy results of the 38th parallel had spread its effects to all corners of Korea. On November 1, 1946, the *Representative Democratic Council of South Korea,* headed by Rhee, issued an appeal to the United Nations; stating (in part):

The arbitrary division of our country with the military forces of the United States in the South and of the Union of Soviet

---

[15] McCune, *op. cit.,* p. 72.
[16] Quoted in Henry Chung, *The Russians Came to Korea* (Washington: The Korean Pacific Press, 1947), p. 101.

Socialist Republics in the North is paralyzing the economy and the people of Korea.

This intolerable condition constitutes a direct threat not only to the peace of the Orient but to the peace of the whole world. It contains every element of international disaster to a world still in the throes of misery resulting from World War II. . . . With the approach of winter, the situation daily grows more perilous. Needed supplies from northern Korea, particularly coal, are not permitted into southern Korea. Needed foodstuffs from the South are denied movement into the North. You, who aim to insure world peace, surely must realize that cold and starvation are always and everywhere the foes of law and order.

The Korean people view with increasing dismay growing inflation, utterly inadequate housing, the care of more than 100,000 refugees from the North, and the denial of the right to trade with other nations. . . .[17]

The *Council* specifically called for the immediate enforcement of the Cairo Declaration and Potsdam Declaration assuring the Korean people of their freedom and independence. The *Council* also asked for the withdrawal of American and Russian forces from Korea and admission of the interim Korean government, being formed under the American military government, into the United Nations. Louise Yim, who had been commissioned to present the petition to the international organization, found, however, that she could not get any official member of the United Nations to sponsor it. The petition was not formally presented to the General Assembly.[18]

In the meantime, General Hodge wrote new letters to General Chistiakov in the north, formally proposing that the Joint Commission be reconvened to take up again the

[17] *Source Material on Korean Politics and Ideologies,* pp. 79-81.
[18] Yim, *op. cit.,* pp. 254-264.

problem of unification of the country. The Soviet commander replied in the negative, reiterating the Russians'
opposition to those Korean leaders "who have compromised
themselves by actively voicing opposition to the Moscow decisions." On December 28, 1946, a year after the Moscow
conference, the State Department once more hopefully repeated that the United States was ready "to sit down with
the Russians at any time to try again to work out under the
Moscow Agreement an acceptable formula for turning
Korea over to the Koreans." [19]

The Korean impasse continued until the spring of 1947.
Then, following an exchange of letters between George C.
Marshall, the new Secretary of State, and Soviet Foreign
Minister Molotov, the problem of reconvening the Joint
Commission received favorable impetus. After making several proposals on the subject, Secretary Marshall in a letter
on May 2, 1947, suggested to Molotov that if the Koreans
who had previously opposed trusteeship were ready to cooperate with the Commission, they should not be excluded
from discussions. Molotov's response, in a letter dated May
7, 1947, took no exception to this principle and it appeared
to the State Department that the Russians had made an
important concession to the viewpoint that "the only people who could be excluded were those people who we both
agreed should be excluded."

As a result, on May 20, 1947, the Joint Commission was
reconvened in Seoul for its second and final effort to unify
the peninsula. As the new discussions got smoothly underway, the American delegation began to hope that an agreement was at hand. By early July, however, this hope was
shattered when the Soviet delegation suddenly reverted to
its old position, rejecting all consultations with those Kore-

[19] *The New York Times,* December 29, 1946.

ans who had expressed opposition to the Moscow Agreement.

The reasons for the Russian reversal can be found in the tremendous developments which had been taking place in American foreign policy. After eighteen months of indecision, the United States launched its containment policy, first enunciated by President Truman on March 12, 1947, in his offer of aid to Greece and Turkey. The Truman Doctrine was followed on June 5, 1947, by Secretary Marshall's famed European reconstruction proposal—the Marshall plan. The war-ravaged nations of western Europe were especially stirred by the proposed Marshall program. The stirrings reverberated in Moscow and all the way to Seoul.

These American foreign policy developments probably were the reason for the drastic change in tactics by the Asian Communists who, according to a State Department analyst, were ordered to forget the "coalition" plan of seizing power and to adopt a new, revolutionary plan of armed activity.[20] In Korea, these events brought about a permanent deadlock in the Joint Soviet-American Commission, and the country approached its second year of unnatural division.

[20] *South Asia in the World Today,* Phillips Talbot, ed. (Chicago: University of Chicago, 1951), p. 206.

# 5

# Enter the United Nations and
# Formation of Two Korean Governments

THE FAILURE of the Joint Commission, which continued its futile meetings in Seoul through the summer and fall of 1947, sent the problem of Korean independence and unification back to Washington and Moscow. While General Hodge now undertook to speed up "the Koreanization" of the military government, the United States came up with a new proposal.

In a letter to Soviet Foreign Minister Molotov on August 28, 1947, the State Department proposed that, in view of the Commission stalemate, a four-power conference be convened in Washington to discuss the entire Korean problem. The Department also forwarded a United States suggestion for holding early elections in both zones to establish zonal legislatures which could, in turn, elect representatives to a national provisional legislature to meet in Seoul to form a united Korea.

On September 4 Molotov replied that Russia could not agree to four-power talks "inasmuch as the Joint Commission is still far from exhausting all its possibilities for working out agreed recommendations which is entirely possible."[1] However, the Russians continued to pursue their old arguments about the Commission deadlock, placing the blame entirely on the Americans, who had insisted "on

[1] U.S. Congress, Senate, *The United States and the Korean Problem*, pp. 4-6.

extending an invitation to groups which had opposed the Moscow decision."[2]

The United States now decided to make a major move to break the stalemate. After receiving Molotov's refusal to go ahead with four-power discussions, the State Department informed the Russians that the United States intended to refer the entire problem of Korea's independence to the forthcoming session of the U.N. General Assembly. On September 17, 1947, Secretary of State George Marshall appeared before the General Assembly and, after discussing the Korean impasse and the tribulations of the Joint Commission, stated:

It appears evident that further attempts to solve the Korean problem by means of bilateral negotiations will only serve to delay the establishment of an independent, united Korea.

It is therefore the intention of the United States government to present the problem of Korean independence to this session of the General Assembly. Although we shall be prepared to submit suggestions as to how the early attainment of Korean independence might be effected, we believe that this is a matter which now requires the impartial judgement of the other members. We do not wish to have the inability of two powers to reach agreement delay any further the urgent and rightful claims of the Korean people to independence.[3]

The American plan was, from the Russian viewpoint, the worst thing that could happen, since it would bring the international body into the picture and perhaps frustrate permanently their efforts to gain control of the country. On September 26, nine days after Marshall's presentation, the Russians offered a substitute proposal, recommending that

[2] *Pravda*, September 11, 1947. See Soviet Press Translations (Seattle: Far Eastern Institute, University of Washington, 1946–1953). Hereafter Soviet Press references will be referred to only by publication and date.

[3] U.S. Congress, Senate, *The United States and the Korean Problem*, pp. 10-11.

all foreign troops leave Korea beginning in 1948 and thus allow the Koreans to erect their own government.

This Russian proposal on troop withdrawal was first made by the Soviet delegation to the Joint Commission in Seoul. When no American answer was received, Molotov amplified the matter in a letter to Marshall on October 9. There was, of course, good reason for the United States' silence, since the Soviet plan appeared, on the surface, to be a popular solution to the entire question. However, the Americans recognized that withdrawal of the occupation forces would leave the South Koreans at the mercy of the militarized, Sovietized north. The State Department rejected the Russian plan, and Secretary Marshall informed Molotov that troop withdrawal constituted only one aspect of the Korean problem.[4]

Meanwhile, Moscow was reacting angrily to the plan to place the Korean question before the United Nations. The government newspaper, *Izvestia*, attacking the United States for refusing to join Russia in withdrawal of troops, declared: "The appeal of the U.S.A. to the United Nations General Assembly, despite the obligations previously incurred, is an attempt to mask its expansionist policy and to conceal its unilateral schemes (previously concocted and long since put into effect), by using the authority of the international organization."[5] This and other statements made it clear the Russians would fight the United States proposal in the United Nations.

Early in November 1947, the United States formally laid the matter before the international body. A U.N. committee heard the American delegation recommend the establishment of a United Nations Commission to oversee an elec-

[4] State Department, *The Conflict in Korea* (Washington: Government Printing Office, 1951), p. 15.
[5] *Izvestia*, October 2, 1947.

tion in Korea to create a representative government, which would then negotiate for the withdrawal of American and Russian troops. The Soviet delegation, led by Andrei A. Gromyko, introduced a counter-resolution, calling for Soviet and American troops to leave Korea by the end of the year so as to allow the Koreans to set up a government "without foreign intervention." The Russian proposal was voted down; the American plan won approval.

On November 13 Gromyko, in a speech to the U.N. Assembly, strenuously opposed the impending intervention of the United Nations, and he warned that the U.S.S.R. would not take part in voting on the resolution. John Foster Dulles, then an adviser to the State Department, argued the United States position before the Assembly, urging adoption of the resolution.

The next day, November 14, 1947, the General Assembly voted forty-three to zero, with six abstentions, to inject itself into the Korean peninsula. In an important resolution the Assembly created a United Nations Temporary Commission on Korea to observe free and secret elections, and recommended these elections be held not later than March 31, 1948, on the basis of adult suffrage and by secret ballot, with the goal of choosing a national assembly. The Assembly also recommended that, immediately after establishment of a national government, arrangements be made with the occupying powers for a complete withdrawal of their armed forces from Korea.

The United States, through the decision of the U.N., had won an important victory. Yet a major obstacle remained, to be discovered by the U.N. Temporary Commission after it had traveled to Seoul, in January 1948, to begin its work. Immediately upon arrival the Commission dispatched letters to commanders of both occupation zones, asking permission to pay courtesy calls. The letter to the Soviet commander in Pyongyang brought no answer. Thereupon the Commission's acting chairman sent a message back to the U.N., asking that the Soviet delegation be requested to seek permission from Moscow for the proposed courtesy call. The Soviet delegation responded to this query with a reminder "of the negative attitude taken by the Soviet government toward the establishment of the United Nations Commission on Korea" and thereby refused any action on the matter.[6]

The Russians' "negative attitude" appeared to have made meaningless the Assembly's stand. Subsequent efforts of the Commission to obtain access to the tightly held northern area were equally unsuccessful, and the unhappy group reported back to the United Nations Interim Committee that it had been unable to carry out its mission because of the attitude of the Soviet authorities in Korea.

It was obvious that without Russian cooperation, there would be no nationwide elections in Korea. Rhee, who had expressed doubts about getting Soviet cooperation, now urged the United Nations to go ahead with separate elections in the south. The Temporary Commission, on February 11, 1948, queried the U.N. body on whether it should go ahead and observe elections in that part of Korea occupied by the United States. *The New York Times*, in an editorial, urged such a course:

We do not see how the United Nations can abandon Korea now to inevitable war. Hard as it is, the choice should be made to go ahead with elections and establishment of a government in South Korea. Then the twenty million people of that area—two-thirds of Korea's population—at least will have a fighting

[6] *The New York Times*, January 24, 1948.

chance to maintain order and develop their country along democratic lines once occupation forces are withdrawn.[7]

The United States government decided that there was no other choice, and the American representative to the United Nations urged the Interim Committee to proceed with elections where they were possible. Acting upon this, on February 28, 1948, the U.N. Committee adopted a resolution directing the Temporary Commission in Seoul to observe elections in the area accessible to it. Several days later the Commission announced it would monitor South Korean elections, to be held not later than May 10, 1948.[8]

The reaction of the Russians and their North Korean allies to this unexpected development was loud and clamorous. Kim Il Sung, already hailed as leader of the North Korean regime, called upon South Korean sympathizers to launch a movement to disrupt separate elections. Kim attacked the Temporary Commission, complaining that it had brought "only disaster and unhappiness to Korea." He charged the United States with deliberately disrupting the Joint Soviet-American Commission, tearing up the Moscow Agreement, violating the Potsdam accord, all the while "scheming to colonize Korea." [9] In Moscow, the Communist Party paper, *Pravda*, declared the Americans, by advocating separate elections, "have openly demonstrated their intention to dismember Korea," and that the Interim Committee resolution was part of an over-all plan for the transformation of southern Korea ". . . into a base for American expansion in the Far East." *Pravda* predicted that the

[7] *Ibid.*, February 13, 1948.
[8] State Department, *Korea 1945 to 1948* (Washington: Government Printing Office, 1948), pp. 70-71.
[9] *The New York Times*, March 12, 1948.

"so-called elections" in southern Korea would be exposed.[10]

The Temporary Commission proceeded with its plans and, as the election date neared, the Communists stepped up their harassing tactics. *Izvestia*, on April 14, carried a Tass dispatch from North Korea claiming a popular movement was "spreading throughout the country against holding separate elections in Southern Korea." North Korean political groups, Tass reported, had appealed to all parties of South Korea to unite with them in opposing the elections.[11]

The Communist appeal fell on sympathetic ears in the south. Many prominent non-Communist Koreans sincerely felt that separate elections would mean the final and complete split of Korea into two separate governments and zones. Among these were Kim Koo and Kim Kiusic, associates of Rhee in the exiled Provisional Government. Both men traveled to Pyongyang where, on April 19, the Communist call for united opposition to separate elections resulted in a "Unity Conference." Afterward, the two Kims returned to Seoul * and issued a joint statement opposing the elections and announcing adherence to the "Unity Conference" declaration, which called for: (a) withdrawal of the two occupation armies; (b) the organization of a provisional government by a national political conference immediately afterwards; and (c) the adoption of a national constitution and the formation of a united national government through a national election.[12]

Despite this important southern opposition and Com-

10 *Pravda*, March 18, 1948.
11 *Izvestia*, April 14, 1948.
* Kim Koo's influence dwindled greatly after his visit to Pyongyang. In the summer of 1949 he was assassinated, reportedly by a member of his own party.
12 *Source Materials on Korean Politics and Ideologies*, pp. 95-96.

munist rumblings that violence would occur, the elections took place in South Korea on schedule. Approximately 95 per cent of the registrants—or 75 per cent of all eligible voters—reportedly voted.[13] When the ballots had been counted, the political forces led by Rhee had won a decisive victory.

The leftists and others charged that the elections had been a fraud, conducted in an atmosphere of police terror. However, the final report of the Temporary Commission was that the elections were "a valid expression of the free will of the electorate in those parts of Korea which were accessible to the Commission and in which the inhabitants constitute approximately two-thirds of the people of all Korea." [14] Another view of the elections, stated George McCune, was that they were "not in fact a free expression of the Korean will," since the observations of the Temporary Commission, with a staff of only about thirty persons, were limited.[15] But as the first genuine popular election in all of Korea's history, it is difficult to criticize the conclusions of the Commission.

The die was cast. On May 27, 1948, the newly elected delegates to the National Assembly of South Korea held a meeting in Seoul and named Rhee as temporary chairman. The Assembly formally convened at 2 P.M., May 31, with the then seventy-three-year-old Rhee proudly proclaiming to the world that "the Government born of this Assembly will be the sovereign, independent government of the entire nation." [16] With Rhee's declaration in mind, the Assembly adopted a resolution inviting the North Koreans to elect

[13] McCune, *op. cit.*, p. 227.
[14] U.S. Congress, Senate, *The United States and the Korean Problem*, pp. 12-24.
[15] McCune, *op. cit.*, p. 229.
[16] *The New York Times*, May 31, 1948.

representatives under the terms of the United Nations resolution, to fill one hundred seats left vacant in the Assembly
for them.

The organization of the South Korean government proceeded swiftly. On July 12, a constitution was adopted proclaiming Korea to be a democratic republic. Eight days
later the Assembly elected Rhee as its first President and,
on August 15, 1948, sovereign authority was transferred
from the United States military government to the Republic of Korea. On that day, the *New York Times* correspondent in Seoul reported that the people greeted the rebirth
of their country "with enthusiasm matched only by that
which swept the country on her liberation from Japan
three years ago."[17] The United States government promptly
took steps to grant diplomatic recognition to the new government and President Truman named John J. Muccio as
special United States representative to Korea, with the rank
of ambassador.[18]

Faced with a *fait accompli* in the south, the Russians
turned their attention to the further communization of
North Korea. On August 15, 1948—the same day that the
Republic of Korea was being officially proclaimed—elections were reportedly held in the north to the Supreme
People's Assembly of Korea. The North Koreans claimed
that a concurrent election was also held clandestinely in
South Korea, thereby making *their* Assembly the legal body
for the entire country. *Pravda* later claimed 77.48 "of all
the electorate" in South Korea had participated in these
elections, despite the "brutal persecution and terror employed by the American occupation authorities and Korean reactionaries."[19]

[17] *Ibid.,* August 16, 1948.
[18] The United States formally recognized the Republic of Korea on
January 1, 1949.
[19] *Pravda,* September 13, 1948.

The creation of the People's Assembly was followed by the establishment of a North Korean government under the leadership of Kim Il Sung. On September 3, the North Korean government adopted a "Constitution of the Democratic Republic of Korea." Several weeks later, addressing a letter to Stalin, Kim requested the Soviet Union to establish diplomatic relations with his government and to exchange ambassadors. On October 12, 1948, in his reply, Stalin announced that the Soviet Union was "ready" to establish such diplomatic relations.[20] General Shtikov was named Russian ambassador. Several other Communist East European nations shortly followed Russia's lead in establishing formal diplomatic relations with the North Korean regime.

So it was that, by the end of the third year of the Russian-American occupation, a Korean nightmare—the creation of two native governments—had come to pass. Kim Kiusic, the Korean leader who had traveled to Pyongyang in opposition to the South Korean elections, and who later disappeared into North Korea, had warned Temporary Commission members that once a South Korean unilateral government had been formed, the Communists in the north under the Soviet Union would establish a separate People's Republic. "Then," prophesized Kim, "you will have two unilateral governments in this little space of something over eighty-five thousand square miles. Not only that, but once such a thing occurs in history, it will go down forever, and it will be perpetuated; then you are responsible and we are responsible for the division of Korea into a northern half and a southern half. . . ."[21]

[20] *Ibid.*, October 13, 1948.
[21] McCune, *op. cit.*, pp. 226-227.

# 6

## Withdrawal of the Russian and
## American Occupation Forces

Two Korean governments vied for the right to rule the entire country. However, only the northern regime was strong, and it now launched a campaign guided by Moscow to bring about the withdrawal of United States forces from Korea. The campaign was initiated with an appeal to both the United States and Russia to withdraw their forces. From the North Korean capital of Pyongyang a Communist radio broadcast derided as "absurd" the expressed fears that such a withdrawal would lead to social disorder and civil war.[1] *Pravda,* on September 14, 1948, published the full text of the North Korean appeal, excerpts as follows:

The Supreme People's Assembly of Korea appeals to the government of the United States and to the government of the Soviet Union, earnestly requesting the immediate and simultaneous withdrawal of their troops from Korea, inasmuch as this is the foremost prerequisite for the unification of Korea, for its economic, political and cultural revival. . . . Assertions to the effect that the simultaneous withdrawal of all foreign troops might lead to disorder and even civil war are utterly groundless and offensive to the national dignity of the Korean people.[2]

Moscow, a few days later, "having considered this appeal," promptly announced that Soviet troops would be

[1] *The New York Times,* September 12, 1948.
[2] *Pravda,* September 14, 1948.

84

entirely withdrawn from Korea by the end of December 1948.[3]

This entire maneuver caught American diplomatic circles by surprise, since the Americans had felt that the Russians would not take such a step in view of the United States' adamant stand against withdrawal. The Soviet announcement, coming on the eve of the opening of the U.N. General Assembly in Paris, also served to throw upon the United States the onus of keeping occupation troops in Korea. The State Department responded on September 20, 1948, with a press release in which it agreed with the Russians that the best interests of the Korean people would be served by a withdrawal of all occupying forces in accordance with the United Nations resolution of November 14, 1947. However, said the State Department:

The United States Government regards the question of the withdrawal of occupying forces as but one facet of the entire question of the unity and independence of Korea. The General Assembly of the United Nations has taken cognizance of this larger question as evidenced by the resolution referred to above, and it may be expected to give further consideration to the matter at its forthcoming meeting.[4]

But the initiative remained with the Russians. The Soviet press hailed the withdrawal announcement, reporting "greatest jubilation" in Korea and "fervent expressions of nationwide gratitude" on the part of the people. In a dispatch from Pyongyang, Tass reported that the Soviet announcement had created confusion in the South Korean Assembly: "A number of deputies demanded the withdrawal of American troops from Korea, declaring that the Korean people will be able . . . to settle the question of the unification of the country." [5]

[3] State Department, *Korea 1945 to 1948*, pp. 114-115.
[4] *Ibid.*, p. 116.
[5] *Izvestia*, September 25, 1948.

The tantalizing Russian announcement shook the weak South Korean government, which feared a United States withdrawal. Lee Bum Suk, the South Korean prime minister, charged that the main purpose of the Soviet announcement was "to stimulate the people of South Korea to agitate for the withdrawal of U.S. Forces." [6] The Americans, however, were proceeding slowly. On September 28, in an official note to the Soviet Union, the United States reasserted that it regarded "the question of troop withdrawal as part of the larger question of Korean unity and independence," and that it would present its views at the appropriate time to the U.N. General Assembly.[7]

To exert added pressure, the Communists now provoked armed insurrection in the South. During October an uprising took place among South Korean Constabulary troops in Cholla-Namdo province on Korea's southwest coast. President Rhee charged that the Communists were infiltrating from the north with orders to foment disorder and he called the Korean cabinet into emergency session to explore plans for the suppression of the uprisings. By the close of the month forces loyal to the Rhee government were able to put down the revolt. On November 2, 1948, however, a second revolt broke out at Taegu among other Constabulary troops. It was also suppressed, but not before fourteen persons were killed. On November 13 Rhee declared martial law in one-fourth of South Korea.

Into this troubled situation was spread the disturbing news that the United States Army was indeed preparing to withdraw from Korea. Severely shaken by this story, the South Korean Assembly convened on November 20, 1948, and adopted an urgent resolution "acknowledging the necessity" for American troops to remain in Korea until

[6] *The New York Times*, September 25, 1948.
[7] State Department, *Korea 1945 to 1948*, pp. 115-116.

the national defense force was sufficiently strong to protect the country. It was this resolution which provoked *Pravda* to a new and bitter attack against the South Korean government and particularly against Rhee, who was charged with being a "traitor" to his country, a "puppet" and "foreign agent and patron of landowners." [8]

The United States called a halt to its unannounced reductions of American forces in Korea. Ambassador Muccio and Major General John B. Coulter, who succeeded Hodge in August 1948, assured the Koreans that there had been no change in United States policy concerning withdrawal of American troops.

The struggle shifted to Paris, where the General Assembly reconvened early in December 1948. After receiving and considering the reports of the U.N. Temporary Commission and Interim Committee on the South Korean elections, the U.N. adopted a new resolution on December 12, over the strenuous opposition of the Soviet bloc. This resolution:

1. Approved the conclusions of the U.N. Temporary Commission.

2. Declared that there had been established a lawful government in South Korea, in that part of the peninsula where the Commission was able to observe and consult with the inhabitants; that the elections in South Korea were "a valid expression of the free will of the electorate of that part of Korea" and that this government was the only such government in Korea.

3. Recommended that the occupying powers should withdraw their occupation forces from Korea as early as practicable.

4. Established a permanent U.N. Commission on Korea

[8] *Pravda*, December 6, 1948.

(UNCOK) to continue the work of the Temporary Commission.

5. Called upon the member states to cooperate with the Commission in bringing about "the complete independence and unity of Korea." [9]

The resolution, approved overwhelmingly by a vote of forty-eight to six, was another victory of a sort for United States policy, but it did not solve the main problem of Soviet noncooperation. This fact soon was made clear to the new U.N. Commission on Korea. After traveling to Seoul, the Commission found that it also, like its predecessor, was shut out of North Korea. A new plea from the U.N. to Moscow to lend its "good offices" in establishing contact with the North Korean government went unanswered.

As the fourth year of the occupation began, the situation regarding the occupation forces was this: (1) the Russians had announced they were withdrawing their troops; (2) the United Nations had recommended that the occupying powers withdraw as early as practicable; (3) the South Korean government had requested that American troops remain; and (4) the United States government now reached a final decision to withdraw completely.

First indications of the American plan was the announcement on December 28, 1948, of the withdrawal of one full American infantry division. Two days later Moscow radio reported that all Soviet troops had left Korea. If true, this left the Americans the only foreign troops in the peninsula, a fact the Russians continued to emphasize in their propaganda broadcasts. On January 11, 1949, *Izvestia* attacked the continued American occupation, arguing that it

---

[9] U.S. Congress, Senate, *The United States and the Korean Problem*, pp. 24-26.

was the "principal obstacle" in the way of the unification of Korea.[10] Although such action would fall in with Moscow's wish, the United States continued to plan for withdrawal.

It should be noted that American withdrawal accorded with American desires. Almost from the day United States troops entered South Korea and found themselves facing a hostile Russian army to the north, fears had arisen of being "mouse-trapped" in the peninsula. Strategically, as far as the United States was concerned, Korea was insignificant. The Joint Chiefs of Staff had no long-term plans for Korean occupation, and the Army wanted to get out.

As early as May 7, 1947, Under Secretary of War Robert P. Patterson formally urged the United States to withdraw, stressing to Secretary of State Marshall the expense of the occupation and Korea's strategic insignificance (to the United States). *The Forrestal Diaries* show that Marshall did not immediately agree with these views.[11] On September 25, 1947, the Joint Chiefs, after careful study, also reported that the United States had little strategic interest in maintaining troops and bases in Korea. Several days later Marshall reported that he was "giving close study to the question of getting out of Korea," that to many people in the State Department it seemed that the Russian offer to withdraw (made on September 18, 1947, in Seoul) might be an opportunity. In response to a question from the former ambassador to Russia, Averell Harriman, as to whether the United States "could get out without loss of face," Marshall replied that that was the aspect of the problem he was giving most serious thought.[12]

[10] *Izvestia*, January 11, 1949.
[11] *The Forrestal Diaries*, Walter Millis, ed. (New York: The Viking Press, 1951), p. 273.
[12] *Ibid.*, pp. 321-322.

The decision on withdrawal was delayed through 1948 as the diplomatic maneuverings led to the U.N. action and creation of the South Korean Republic. Toward the end of 1948, the gradual reduction of United States forces already mentioned took place. In February 1949, the United States announced to the United Nations that it would defer the withdrawal fo its remaining troops at the request of the Republic of Korea.[13] However, planning for the withdrawal was initiated. General MacArthur, who had been asked for his opinion, concurred in the plan, and in March 1949, the American government approved the withdrawal.

The task of making the first public announcement was given to President Rhee. On April 18, 1949, Rhee issued a statement in which he proclaimed that South Korea's forces were

rapidly approaching the point at which our security can be assured, provided the Republic of Korea is not called upon to face attack from a foreign source. Discussions, therefore, are now underway between representatives of the Republic of Korea and of the United States concerning the establishment of a date in the course of several months for the withdrawal from Korea of U.S. troops.[14]

Not everyone felt the American decision was wise. Doubt was expressed by the Philippine representative on the U.N. Commission, Rufino Lunna, who declared he was strongly opposed to United States withdrawal. Lunna said he was convinced that the Korean republic would be unable to defend itself against attack. At his request, therefore, the Commission adopted a resolution on May 23, 1949, disclaiming any responsibility "for the timing or the facili-

[13] *Nippon Times,* February 26, 1949.
[14] *The New York Times,* April 19, 1949.

tating of the withdrawal of the forces of the occupying powers." [15]

On June 7, 1949—while American troops were packing their belongings—President Truman recommended to Congress that there be a continuation of economic assistance to South Korea. On June 8 the State Department issued a press release which discussed the United States plan for economic and technical aid to Korea, and plans for establishing a United States military training program and transfer of military equipment to the South Koreans. The release added that:

In pursuance of the recommendation contained in the General Assembly's Resolution of December 12, 1948, to the effect that the occupying Powers should "withdraw their occupation forces from Korea as early as practicable," the United States Government will soon have completed the withdrawal of its occupation forces from that country. As is clear from the broad program of assistance outlined . . . this withdrawal in no way indicates a lessening of United States interest in the Republic of Korea, but constitutes rather another step toward the normalization of relations with that Republic. . . .[16]

So did the Americans convince themselves that it was economically, politically, and militarily desirable to withdraw their forces. How events would have transpired had they remained in Korea will never be known. On June 29, 1949, the last of the American troops departed, leaving behind some five hundred members of the United States Military Advisory Group. Even as the last increment of eight thousand American troops sailed from Inchon, the U.N. Commission watched as South Korean troops bat-

[15] *Ibid.*, May 23, 1949.
[16] U.S. Congress, Senate, *The United States and the Korean Problem,* pp. 26-27.

tled "northern invaders" on the Ongjin peninsula just northwest of Seoul. In a report to the U.N., the Commission noted that one of its subcommittees toured the "front lines," passing howitzer batteries and observing an artillery duel and machine gun fire from both sides.[17]

The summer of 1949 was the first summer in half-a-century that the Koreans were alone in their peninsula—free of foreign armies. But their occupiers had left behind a horrible legacy and the Koreans looked across the 38th parallel at each other, fingering their weapons.

[17] *The New York Times,* June 29, 1949.

# 7

## The March to "Civil" War

I<small>N THE</small> early summer of 1949 the United States was engaged in more than a withdrawal from Korea; it was engaged in a complete withdrawal from the mainland of Asia. During 1949 the State Department was putting the final touches to its famous "White Paper on China," which noted that "the heart of China" was in Communist hands and took the position that only full-scale intervention by the United States with land, sea, and air forces could have saved the situation for the discredited Nationalist Government of the Republic of China (Kuomintang). The Communists, about to conquer the whole of China, seemed to be riding a relentless tide of victory, and Korea, as in her long past, would be greatly influenced by the tremendous developments on the mainland.

The presence in South Korea of the few Americans of the military advisory group continued to be the target of Communist propaganda attack. The remaining Americans, according to the Russians, had "aroused righteous indignation" among the masses of South Korea.[1] The North Korean regime also demanded the ouster of the Americans.

In the north subterfuge was being mixed with stepped-up military activity. On July 6, the North Korean radio reported that the Pyongyang government would sponsor nationwide elections on September 5, 1949, to create a unified legislature for the entire country. This legislature

[1] *Izvestia,* July 2, 1949.

would then create an all-Korean government which, the
Communists said, would be free from the control of the
United States, the Soviet Union, and the United Nations.[2]
While thus talking of peaceful elections, which were never
held, the North Koreans simultaneously stepped up har-
assment raids along the 38th parallel. These skirmishes
and fire-fights provided the North Korean armies with invaluable combat experience, as well as military intelligence on the capabilities of the South Korean Constabulary.

From Seoul the U.N. Commission reported to the General Assembly on July 28, 1949, that "embittered propaganda and hostile activities which now mark the relations
between the two parts of Korea render the prospect of unification more and more remote." The Commission said
that, like its predecessor, it was unable to forward the objectives of the General Assembly, in view of the world wide
antagonism existing between Russia and the United States,
and Russian obstructionism in Korea.[3]

While this discouraging report was being studied at
Lake Success, the North Korean regime launched another
invasion of the Ongjin peninsula with an estimated six
thousand troops. The fighting flared for several days, with
the South Koreans claiming the invaders were repulsed,
although they admitted the Communists held two points
inside the southern boundary.[4] As summer faded, the situation along the parallel deteriorated to such an extent that
the U.N. Commission warned the General Assembly, on
September 8, 1949, of the growing possibility of full-scale,
"barbarous civil war" in the peninsula. "On both sides of
the thirty-eighth parallel," reported the Commission,

[2] *The New York Times,* July 8, 1949.
[3] *Source Materials on Korean Politics and Ideologies,* pp. 132-133.
[4] *The New York Times,* August 6, 1949.

"there is much military posturing. This holds a serious danger of provoking open military conflict." [5]

On October 14, 1949, in letters to U.N. Secretary-General Trygve Lie and Carlos P. Romulo, the president of the General Assembly, the North Korean government openly and clearly announced its intention to reunite Korea by force. The letters stated:

The government of the Korean People's Democratic Republic deems it necessary to declare that should the United Nations ignore in the future the will and strivings of the Korean people, considering only the selfish interest of a small group of traitors and betrayers of the Korean people, the Korean people will not abandon the struggle and will reserve for itself the right to continue by measures at its disposal the struggle for . . . removal of UNCOK and for final unification of the country by its own forces into a united democratic state.[6]

This Communist threat failed to deter the General Assembly from once more considering the problem of Korea. On October 21 the Assembly voted to continue the Commission (UNCOK), charging the Commission members with the additional responsibility of investigating and reporting developments which might lead to military conflict in the area.[7]

The persistency of the international body did not sit well with the North Korean authorities. Their reaction took the form of a new organization, called the "United Democratic Fatherland Front of Korea." This Communist organization proceeded to denounce the United Nations, declaring the Assembly had "blindly subjugated itself to

[5] *Ibid.*, September 9, 1949.
[6] *Ibid.*, October 18, 1949.
[7] U.S. Congress, Senate, *The United States and the Korean Problem*, pp. 28-29.

the dictation of the American imperialists." The Central Committee of the "Fatherland Front" further warned:

There is no place in our country for uninvited guests who are a menace to the sovereignty of the Korean people. We call upon all patriotic parties and public organizations, as in the past, to boycott the United Nations Commission, as well as to use every method to impede the activity of the Commission which is directed against the interests of the Korean people. . . . The forces of our people are great and their aspiration for unity and independence is unshakeable. Neither the bayonets of Syngman Rhee bands, nor the threats of the foreign imperialists can stop them. Korea shall be united and independent.[8]

Around the "Fatherland Front" the Communists sought to rally all dissident elements in the south. Pyongyang radio, throughout the winter of 1949–50, continually urged the South Koreans to rise in rebellion. The Communists claimed that 77,000 southern partisans, in September 1949 alone, had engaged the Rhee forces in 1184 clashes.[9] Praise was heaped on the dissidents as the Communists began to activate all their various apparatus aimed at subversion and conquest.

What was the United States doing while the Korean pot began to boil? On the diplomatic level, the United States government continued to support the activities of the United Nations in its watchdog role in Korea. On the military level, American policy was clearly outlined by Secretary of State Dean Acheson in a speech on January 12, 1950, before the National Press Club in Washington, D.C. According to Acheson, who was speaking for the Pentagon, the American defensive perimeter in the Pacific ran from the Aleutians to Japan, the Ryukyus and the Philippines.

[8] *Izvestia,* November 29, 1949.
[9] *Source Materials on Korean Politics and Ideologies,* pp. 133-144.

As for the security of other areas of the Pacific (i.e., Korea), Acheson stated: If an attack occurred, the initial reliance "must be on the people attacked to resist it and then upon the commitments of the entire civilized world under the charter of the United Nations."

What Acheson's statement meant was that Korea was considered to be outside the area in which the United States would automatically react to an aggression. His statement evoked despair and anguish in Seoul,[10] and probably delight in Moscow and Pyongyang.

On the economic level, the United States sought to implement its promise of assistance to South Korea. In January 1950, President Truman requested a congressional authorization of $120 million for Korean aid. In the House of Representatives a coalition of Republicans and southern Democrats rejected the Korean aid bill, in rebuke over the administration's China policy. Secretary Acheson, in a letter to the President on January 20, expressed his "concern and dismay" and warned that "this action, if not quickly repaired, will have the most far-reaching adverse effects upon our foreign policy, not only in Korea but in many other areas of the world." [11] Several weeks later the administration managed to win enough congressional support to pass a "Far Eastern Economic Assistance Bill," which authorized the $120 million short-term Korean aid and also new economic aid to the battered Chinese Nationalist government, which was attempting to regroup its forces on Formosa.

The economic aid had been approved, but it appeared to have little bearing on the actual situation in Korea,

10 Yim, *op. cit.*, pp. 295-296.
11 State Department, *Strengthening the Forces of Freedom, Selected Speeches and Statements of Secretary of State Acheson* (Washington: Government Printing Office, 1950), pp. 174-175.

which lay under the threat of "civil" war. In a similarly unrealistic manner the United States government limited the Republic of Korea's defensive capabilities by limiting the size of the arms supplied to the Constabulary. An estimated $110 million worth of equipment had been left behind by the United States Army when it departed in June 1949, but this consisted mostly of small arms—rifles, pistols, machine guns, mortars, and some bazookas, anti-tank guns, and 105-howitzers.[12] In the north, on the other hand, the Russians had supplied the North Korean Army with heavy equipment, including tanks.

The United States remained, in the spring of 1950, unconcerned with a possible invasion but was increasingly worried over South Korea's critical economic situation. Acheson, early in April 1950, in an *aide-memoire* to the Korean ambassador in Washington, threatened to cut the new Korean economic assistance program unless prompt action was taken by the Republic to solve its mounting inflation. The *aide-memoire* also expressed the United States government's equal concern over reports that the Rhee government intended to postpone the general elections from May 1950, until November.[13] Rhee, as a result of this American pressure, shortly announced that the government was taking steps to remedy the unbalanced budget through taxation and that the elections would be held on May 30. Responding to Rhee's cooperative attitude, the United States Congress voted, on June 5, 1950, to set aside additional funds for Korea economic rehabilitation.

By early June 1950, the Russian-North Korean plans for invasion had been completed. The North Korean armies,

[12] Department of Defense, *Semiannual Report of the Secretary of Defense, January 1 to June 30, 1950* (Washington: Government Printing Office, 1950), p. 15.

[13] *Source Materials on Korean Politics and Ideologies,* pp. 145-146.

officered and guided in important instances by members of the Soviet Red Army, were slowly shifted into position for a rapid advance south.

American intelligence agencies in the Far East became aware of this growing aggressive posture of the North Koreans. On March 10, 1950, General MacArthur's intelligence branch reported to the JCS that there were indications that an invasion of South Korea was planned for June 1950; however, Tokyo evaluated the report as doubtful. On March 25, another Tokyo report was dispatched to Washington stating the belief of American intelligence that there would be no civil war that spring or summer and that, instead, continued guerrilla warfare was likely.[14]

On May 10 a public warning that an invasion was imminent was sounded by the South Korean Defense Minister, who told the press that his intelligence reports indicated the North Koreans were moving in force toward the 38th parallel.[15] The Pentagon authorities, however, in evaluating the incoming reports, agreed with MacArthur's estimate and decided an attack was not imminent.

Washington's attention remained focused on the Korean elections. These were duly held, and resulted in strong gains for the independents at the expense of President Rhee's supporters. The losses experienced by Rhee's party were a significant refutation of the charge that South Korea was a completely intimidated state, at the mercy of Rhee's police and strong-arm squads. The voters seemed to have had complete freedom in the elections.

Meanwhile, American diplomatic and military leaders

[14] U.S. Congress, Senate, *Military Situation in the Far East,* Hearing before Committee on Armed Services and Committee on Foreign Relations, U.S. Senate, 82d Cong. 1st Sess. on military situation in the Far East and the facts surrounding the relief of General MacArthur (Washington: Government Printing Office, 1951), p. 1990.

[15] *The New York Times,* May 10, 1950.

were visiting the Far East on various missions. John Foster Dulles, representing the State Department in discussions in Tokyo of a Japanese peace treaty, flew to Korea and toured the 38th parallel. General Omar Bradley, chairman of the Joint Chiefs of Staff, and Secretary of Defense Louis Johnson, arrived in Tokyo on June 18, 1950, to discuss the Far Eastern military situation with MacArthur.[16] In the briefings by the supreme commander and his staff, nothing at all was said to Bradley and Johnson about a possible war in Korea.

Early in June 1950, the North Koreans undertook a last-minute, farcical maneuver to mask their plans. This was initiated by Pyongyang radio, which broadcast a proposal for the holding on August 5, 1950, of a general, all-Korea election. Several days after this broadcast, a second broadcast was heard in Seoul in which the North Korean regime issued an invitation to "all political parties, social organizations and leaders of the southern half as well as the United Nations Commission" to meet at a location on the parallel to receive leaflets urging the nationwide elections.[17]

This belated recognition and invitation to the U.N. Commission was ironic, since the Commission (and its predecessor) had tried for two years to make contact with the North Korean government. The U.N. Commission somewhat pessimistically dispatched a delegate to the appointed place. Three North Koreans appeared, handed the delegate four copies of an election appeal and refused to be drawn into conversation, stating that all they were instructed to do was to pass out the leaflets. The following day their activity south of the parallel was brought to a halt with their arrest by South Korean authorities.

The entire maneuver, whatever its motivation, appeared

---

[16] *Nippon Times*, June 19, 1950.
[17] *The New York Times*, June 11, 1950.

to be unnecessary. The world was paying little heed to Korea. When, in the early morning hours of June 25, the Communist armies launched their general invasion of South Korea, the world's capitals reacted with complete surprise. According to author John Gunther, who was in Tokyo when the invasion began, even the "South Koreans and Americans in Korea, to say nothing of SCAP in Tokyo, were taken utterly by surprise. They were as blankly astonished as if the sun had suddenly gone out." [18]

As the North Korean armies smashed southward, the Communist press and radio immediately churned out the charge that the armies of "the traitor Syngman Rhee" had attacked first and that the North Koreans were merely launching a counterattack. On June 26 Kim Il Sung, in an emotional appeal over Pyongyang radio, called upon his forces to liberate South Korea.

Dear brothers and sisters! Great danger threatens our motherland and its people. What is needed to liquidate this menace? In this war, which is being waged against the Syngman Rhee clique, the Korean people must defend the Korean People's Democratic Republic and its constitution; they must liquidate the unpatriotic fascist puppet regime of Syngman Rhee which has been established in the southern part of the republic; they must liberate the southern part of our motherland from the domination of the Syngman Rhee clique; and they must restore the people's committees there—the real organs of power. Under the banner of the Korean People's Democratic Republic, we must complete the unification of the motherland and create a single, independent, democratic state. The war which we are forced to wage is a just war for the unification and independence of the motherland and for freedom and democracy. . . . [19]

[18] John Gunther, *The Riddle of MacArthur* (New York: Harpers & Brothers, 1950-51), p. 166.
[19] *Pravda,* June 27, 1950.

So the North Koreans, aided and abetted by the Soviets, shattered what little was left of the morning calm and launched the inevitable effort to unify the peninsula by force.

# 8

# Washington Reacts

At 9:26 P.M. Saturday, June 24, Washington time, the first official report of the invasion was received from Ambassador Muccio, who informed the State Department that the Communist attack appeared to constitute "an all-out offensive against the Republic of Korea." [1] In the hours and days following receipt of this message, the unexpected happened in Washington. The leaders of the American government, as the consequences of the North Korean aggression sank in, reversed the United States policy of withdrawal from the Asian mainland. That reversal sent a tremendous tide of change into the future. Its impact on historical events was, and is, incalculable.

Within hours after Muccio's telegram arrived in Washington, the United States diplomatic and defense leaders were summoned to the State Department. A phone call to Secretary Acheson informed him of the invasion. Shortly after midnight Acheson telephoned long-distance to President Truman, who had gone to his home at Independence, Missouri, for a family visit. After discussing the Korean crisis, Truman and Acheson agreed to bring the attack to the attention of the U.N. This was in line with earlier United States planning that, in the event of aggression in Asia, "initial reliance must be on the people attacked to

[1] The Muccio telegram and 100 other documents covering developments in June-July 1950 leading to U.S. and U.N. participation in the Korean conflict are found in the State Department publication, *United States Policy in the Korean Crisis* (Washington: Government Printing Office, 1950).

resist it and then upon the commitments of the entire civilized world under the charter of the United Nations." [2] The U.N. Secretary-General was called and alerted to an appeal to the Security Council.

Later that morning, Acheson phoned the President once more. He emphasized that a world crisis was upon them and that only the President could make the necessary decisions. Truman immediately ordered his plane readied for his return to Washington.

Sunday, June 25, while most Americans turned to their maps to see where Korea was, the Security Council convened in the afternoon at Lake Success. By this time the Council had received an official report from the U.N. Commission confirming the attack and stating that it was assuming the character of full-scale war. The Commission reported a rumor that the North Korean government had broadcast a formal declaration of war. This was later confirmed. [3] The Security Council also had received urgent appeals for aid from the besieged Republic of Korea.

The United States deputy representative to the Council, Earnest Gross, addressed the international body. He summed up developments in Korea from 1945 on and the role played by the United Nations. Then he submitted, on behalf of the United States government, a draft resolution for Council consideration. This resolution was adopted, after minor revision, by a Council vote of nine to zero. (The Soviet Union was absent, having boycotted the Council in protest against the presence of Nationalist China. Yugoslavia abstained.) It declared that the North Korean attack constituted a "breach of the peace" and demanded an immediate end of hostilities and withdrawal of the North Korean army. In addition, the Council called

[2] See Chap. 7, pp. 96-97.
[3] State Department, *United States Policy in the Korean Crisis*, p. 15.

on all its members "to render every assistance to the United Nations in the execution of this resolution and to refrain from giving assistance to the North Korean authorities."

In his plane speeding toward Washington, President Truman was thinking of past aggressions. He later wrote in his memoirs:

I recalled some earlier instances: Manchuria, Ethiopia, Austria. I remembered how each time that the democracies failed to act it had encouraged the aggressors to keep going ahead. Communism was acting in Korea just as Hitler, Mussolini and the Japanese had acted ten, fifteen and twenty years earlier. I felt certain that if South Korea was allowed to fall, Communist leaders would be emboldened to override nations closer to our own shores. . . . If this was allowed to go unchallenged, it would mean a third world war. . . .[4]

It was a resolute President who landed at Washington at 7:20 P.M. June 25, and hurried into a high-level conference at Blair House. In attendance were Acheson, Secretary of Defense Louis Johnson, Secretary of the Army Frank Pace, Jr., Secretary of the Navy Francis P. Matthews, Secretary of the Air Force Thomas K. Finletter, the Joint Chiefs of Staff Generals Omar N. Bradley, J. Lawton Collins, Hoyt S. Vandenberg, Admiral Forrest P. Sherman, and others. In an air of tension and crisis, the American leaders held an almost three-hour discussion on the aggression, the Security Council's resolution, and possible American courses of action.

It was clear to the President and his advisers that the Russians were behind the North Korean attack. The President expressed the opinion that they were trying to get Korea by default, hoping the United States would fear to

[4] Truman, *Years of Trial and Hope*, Memoirs (New York: Doubleday & Co., 1956), p. 333.

intervene. The American leaders strongly felt that the Russian plan must not succeed, but the thought of what it might take to frustrate the Communist effort was disturbing. As the possibilities and probabilities of the dark future were explored, the President and his assistants gave first thoughts to American dependents and noncombatants in the war zone. General MacArthur was authorized to use his air power and navy to prevent the Inchon-Kimpo-Seoul area from falling into unfriendly hands while an evacuation took place. In addition, the President approved a suggestion that American naval and air power be moved from the Philippines and elsewhere toward the danger zone.

The following morning, June 26, Truman issued a statement to the press:

I conferred Sunday evening with the Secretaries of State and Defense, their senior advisers, and the Joint Chiefs of Staff, about the situation in the Far East created by unprovoked aggression against the Republic of Korea.

The Government of the United States is pleased with the speed and determination with which the United Nations Security Council acted to order a withdrawal of the invading forces to positions north of the 38th parallel. In accordance with the resolutions of the Security Council, the United States will vigorously support the effort of the Council to terminate this serious breach of the peace.

Our concern over the lawless action taken by the forces from North Korea, and our sympathy and support for the people of Korea in this situation, are being demonstrated by the cooperative action of American personnel in Korea, as well as by steps taken to expedite and augment assistance of the type being furnished under the Mutual Defense Assistance Program.

Those responsible for this act of aggression must realize how seriously the Government of the United States views such threats to the peace of the world. Willful disregard of the obligation to keep the peace cannot be tolerated by nations that support the United Nations Charter.[5]

Most Americans reading the Presidential statement concluded that the United States would take every action short of war. Meanwhile, the attention of the leaders of the American government remained focused on Korea. There was a vague hope that the Communist forces would, perhaps, heed the Security Council resolution and withdraw. However, it soon became clear that they had no such intention. As the North Korean armies plunged deeper into the Republic of Korea, General MacArthur reported that a complete South Korean collapse was imminent. In Washington opinion crystallized that the United States government must take decisive action.

The night of June 26 the President and his advisers met once more at Blair House. At this meeting, which lasted only an hour, they took another step forward in the reversal of United States policy. Acheson, reading from a prepared statement, recommended to the President that American naval and air power be used to help the South Koreans repel the North Korean attack. The military chiefs supported the State Department recommendation, although there was some discussion of the difficulties that might arise. President Truman thereupon approved the recommendation to go into Korea with American naval and air power.

This decision, as we have indicated, ran counter to all that had gone before. Korea had previously been placed outside the American defense perimeter. Army leaders had agitated for a long time to withdraw from the peninsula, considering Korea untenable in the event of a Soviet attack. They felt, in addition, that in a global war with

[5] State Department, *United States Policy in the Korean Crisis*, pp. 16-17.

Russia, the main adversary, Korea was absolutely the wrong place to fight decisive battles. Yet, despite the conviction that it was wrong to become involved militarily in Korea, that policy was overthrown.

The reason, aside from America's clear moral commitments to Korea, was that the attack, in Acheson's words,

was a challenge to the whole system of collective security, not only in the Far East, but everywhere in the world. It was a threat to all nations newly arrived at independence. . . . This was a test which would decide whether other nations would be intimidated by this show of force.

The decision to meet force with force in Korea was essential. It was the unanimous view of the political and military advisers of the President that this was the right thing to do. . . .[6]

The decision made, that night, June 26, the JCS authorized General MacArthur to use his navy and air force to attack all North Korean military targets south of the 38th parallel, with the objective of clearing South Korea of Communist military forces.[7] The next morning the President informed the world of this action. He declared that the attack on Korea "makes it plain beyond all doubt that Communism has passed beyond the use of subversion to conquer independent nations and will now use armed invasion and war." Truman further stated that he had ordered the Seventh Fleet to prevent a Chinese Communist attack on Formosa, whose future status, he said, "must await the restoration of security in the Pacific, a peace settlement with Japan, or consideration by the United Nations."[8]

On June 27, the day of the President's announcement, there were other important developments on the diplo-

[6] Acheson's testimony, *Military Situation in the Far East,* pp. 1715-1716.
[7] Appendix K, *ibid.,* p. 3192.
[8] State Department, *United States Policy in the Korean Crisis,* p. 18.

matic level. To bolster its stand, the United States sought additional U.N. support. Ambassador Warren Austin, the American representative to the Security Council, told that body that the North Korean authorities had clearly disregarded the decision of the Council, and that the armed invasion of the Republic of Korea continued. Austin called upon the Council to invoke stringent sanctions to restore international peace; he submitted a second United States resolution recommending that members of the U.N. furnish assistance to South Korea to repel the attack and restore international peace. He then read to the Council the President's announcement that United States air and naval power had been ordered into action.[9] The resolution was promptly adopted, by a vote of seven to one, with the Soviet representative still absent and India and Egypt abstaining.[10]

The State Department, meanwhile, sought to keep diplomatic lines open to Moscow. On June 27 the American ambassador in Moscow delivered a note to the Russians, calling their attention to the invasion and requesting the Soviet Union to use its influence with the North Koreans to call off the attack. The American note also asked assurance "that the Union of Soviet Socialist Republics disavows responsibility for this unprovoked and unwarranted attack. . . ."[11] The Department, by taking the public position that the U.S.S.R. was not involved in the attack, hoped to give the Russians the opportunity to get out from under the invasion and to limit its reaction to diplomatic channels.

The rapid-fire developments of June 25-27 must have confounded the Kremlin. The initial Russian response

[9] *Ibid.*

[10] India several days later accepted the resolution. Yugoslavia cast the negative vote.

[11] State Department, *United States Policy in the Korean Crisis*, pp. 63-64.

was to brand the Security Council resolutions as illegal because of the absence of the Soviet Union and Communist China.[12] To the worried State Department, this statement seemed to indicate the Soviets would not enter the conflict.

The American Far East air force and navy went into action to aid the South Korean republic. However, from the air it was difficult to distinguish friend from foe, and few profitable targets were found. Seoul fell to the invaders on June 28 and the South Koreans began a disorganized retreat to the south. The JCS thereupon authorized MacArthur to extend his air and naval attacks into North Korea, but he was cautioned to stay clear of the Manchurian and Soviet borders. The JCS also authorized the use of Army troops "to insure the retention of a port and air base in the general area of Pusan. . . ." [13]

On Thursday, June 29, the third historic American governmental meeting on the Korean crisis was held, this time at the White House.* The problem facing the President and his advisers was how to stop the North Korean army. The use of American troops, touched upon briefly in the previous meetings at Blair House, was now seriously explored. A final decision, however, was withheld pending a report from MacArthur, who had flown to Korea for a firsthand inspection of the battlefront.[14]

In the early morning hours of June 30, Washington time, MacArthur reported to the JCS on his personal reconnaissance. He stated that the South Korean army was in confusion, that supplies and equipment had been aban-

---

[12] The Soviet Union delegate returned, finally, to the Council seat in August.

[13] Appendix K, *Military Situation in the Far East,* p. 3192.

* The White House was being remodeled during this period.

[14] *Nippon Times,* June 30, 1950.

doned or lost, and that the South Koreans were incapable of united action. He further stated that the only assurance of holding the Han River line south of Seoul, and of regaining lost ground, would be through the use of American ground combat forces. Accordingly, MacArthur continued, if authorized, he planned immediately to move a United States regimental combat team to the combat area as the nucleus of a possible building-up of two divisions from Japan for early offensive action, in accordance with his mission of clearing South Korea of North Korean forces.[15]

About 5 A.M. Secretary of the Army Pace phoned the President and relayed MacArthur's report. The President promptly authorized the use of one American regimental combat team. Later that morning the President met again with his advisers. After discussing an offer of 33,000 troops made by Chiang Kai-shek, Truman then decided MacArthur should be given full authority to use the ground forces under his command.

In a subsequent meeting with leaders of Congress, the President reviewed the darkening situation and announced his decision to use American troops. There was no dissent from the group and the President authorized issuance of a statement to the press; its concluding sentence was: "General MacArthur has been authorized to use certain supporting ground units." In the months ahead these units were to grow into an American combat army of more than 210,000 men.

The basic decisions had been made. On July 1, the JCS again instructed MacArthur to be careful that, in establishing a naval blockade of Korea, his forces stayed well clear of the coastal waters of Manchuria and the Soviet Union. On July 4, the American ambassador in Moscow informed

[15] Bradley's testimony, *Military Situation in the Far East*, p. 1112.

the Russians that President Truman had ordered such a blockade of the Korean coast, effective at once, in accordance with the Security Council resolutions. The Russian response several days later was again to denounce the Council's resolutions.

Meanwhile at the U.N., offers of military and economic aid from members slowly trickled in. On July 7, 1950, the Council adopted a third resolution, requesting the various nations supplying forces and other assistance to place them under a unified command headed by the United States. This resolution further requested the United States to designate the commander of such forces. The next day President Truman announced that, in response to the Council's recommendation, he was naming General MacArthur as the commanding general of the unified command.

Thus, in a period of less than two weeks from the day the aggression was initiated, the Russians and North Koreans found themselves facing an impressive array of nations led by the United States. By acting decisively, the United States had ruined a near-perfect plan of conquest.

# 9

## MacArthur's Strategy
## Defeats the North Koreans

Aᴛ ꜰɪʀsᴛ, the Americans of the Eighth Army in Japan, scattered among four understrength divisions, watched with a certain disinterest the electrifying events taking place in Korea. There hadn't been the slightest indication that they would be involved in the war. Their commander, General MacArthur, when first told of the attack belittled its significance, believing that it was just another large-scale reconnaissance by North Korean forces. It is clear, from all the evidence at hand, that neither MacArthur nor his subordinates expected to be called upon for a military effort in the peninsula.

The American detachment, however, was not shared by the Japanese, whose long history had taught them the importance of the Korean peninsula to the peace of northeast Asia. "There is no need for hysteria among the Japanese," a Tokyo newspaper cautioned on June 27, "but there should be a calm appraisal of the situation, for a civil war in Korea represents trouble which is too close for comfort." [1] When, that same day, MacArthur was energized by orders to send the United States navy and air force into action, and American warplanes roared off their Japanese air bases toward Korea, a perceptible sigh of relief swept the Japanese islands.

[1] *Nippon Times,* June 27, 1950.

MacArthur, after later receiving authority to use American ground forces, began what was probably the most successful improvisation in the history of warfare. Noting that the South Korean army was almost disintegrated, he concluded that the Han River line south of Seoul could no longer be held. He therefore issued orders for the establishment of a beachhead in the neighborhood of Pusan, and began flying in troops from Japan, hoping to establish a point of resistance about which he could rally the fast-retreating South Koreans.

The first American foot soldiers came from the 24th Division, under Major General William F. Dean. A special combat team from the division, Task Force Smith (named after Lieutenant Colonel Charles B. Smith), landed at Pusan and was rushed northward by rail and truck to make the first American contact with the enemy on July 5, in the vicinity of Osan. Now followed a series of historic engagements in which the Americans created MacArthur's point of resistance, fighting delaying actions that were "marked by frustration, heroism and death." [2]

The task force, and other elements of the 24th Division which arrived at the scene, lacked the numbers and weapons to defeat the North Koreans, and were decimated. But MacArthur's strategy succeeded. Within fourteen days after first contact with the enemy at Osan, MacArthur was able to report to the Joint Chiefs of Staff that:

With the deployment in Korea of major elements of the Eighth Army now accomplished, the first phase of the campaign has ended and with it the chance of victory by the North Korean forces. The enemy's plan and great opportunity depended upon the speed with which he could overrun South Korea once he had breached the Han River line and with

[2] Department of the Army, Office of the Chief of Military History, *Korea: 1950* (Washington: Government Printing Office, 1952), p. 15.

overwhelming numbers and superior weapons temporarily shattered South Korean resistance. This chance he has now lost through the extraordinary speed with which the Eighth Army has been deployed from Japan to stem his rush. When he crashed the Han line the way seemed entirely open and victory was within his grasp.

The desperate decision to throw in piecemeal American elements as they arrived by every available means of transport from Japan was the only hope to save the situation. The skill and valor thereafter displayed in successive holding actions by the ground forces in accordance with this concept, brilliantly supported in complete coordination by air and naval elements, forced the enemy into continued deployments, costly frontal attacks and confused logistics, which so slowed his advance and blunted his drive that we have bought the precious time necessary to build a secure base.

I do not believe that history records a comparable operation which excelled the speed and precision with which the Eighth Army, the Far East Air Force and the Seventh Fleet have been deployed to a distant land for immediate commitment to major operations. . . .[3]

There now began the task of building up the base at Pusan, where Lieutenant General Walton K. Walker set up Eighth Army headquarters. While men, supplies and equipment began slowly to fill the logistic pipeline to Pusan, the 24th Division was reeling under North Korean blows. In bloody, confusing fighting near Taejon, General Dean and a number of his troops were cut off from retreat. After wandering thirty-five days behind enemy lines, Dean was finally captured, but the outside world learned nothing of this until much later.[4]

In the early weeks of August 1950, the first of three large

---

[3] Appendix PP, *Military Situation in the Far East,* pp. 3381-3382.

[4] Dean told of his Korean captivity in *The Dean Story,* William L. Worden, ed. (New York: The Viking Press, 1954).

contingents of American reinforcements arrived at Pusan after sailing directly from the United States and Hawaii. Soon elements of four United States divisions, a Marine brigade, and five Republic of Korea divisions were deployed in a protective arc around Pusan. These forces dug in to create the famed Pusan perimeter. General Walker, shuttling his units from one critical point to another, succeeded in blunting the repeated North Korean assaults on his lines.

While the battle was joined in the southeast corner of Korea, events were occurring elsewhere which would have important repercussions on the conflict. These related to Formosa. The President's order to the Seventh Fleet to prevent an attack on Formosa apparently forestalled a Chinese Communist invasion plan. On July 29, the Chinese Nationalists gratefully offered to send 33,000 men to Korea to repel the North Korean attack. Secretary of State Acheson, in response, expressed appreciation for the offer but added that:

In light . . . of the threat of invasion of Taiwan by Communist forces from the mainland, a threat repeated in the last day or so by spokesmen of the Chinese Communist regime in Peiping, it is the view of the Government of the United States of America that it would be desirable for representatives of General MacArthur's Headquarters to hold discussions with the Chinese military authorities on Taiwan concerning the plans for the defense of the island against invasion prior to any final decision on the wisdom of reducing the defense forces on Taiwan by transfer of troops to Korea. . . .[5]

MacArthur also was opposed to accepting the Chinese Nationalist offer, believing they would be of little effect in Korea. He suggested he would go himself to Formosa to explain the situation to Chiang Kai-shek. On July 31 the

[5] Appendix PP, *Military Situation in the Far East*, p. 3383.

general flew to Taipeh for this conference. MacArthur's views on the importance of keeping Formosa out of enemy hands were well known; he had imparted them to General Bradley and Secretary of Defense Johnson during their visit to Tokyo just prior to the Korean attack. Now, after his meeting with Chiang Kai-shek, it was agreed that the United States and Nationalist China would coordinate their efforts to defend Formosa and that Chiang's offer of 33,000 troops would be held in abeyance.[6]

The MacArthur visit to Formosa was promptly interpreted by observers as a conflict with the State Department, which had been troubled, in any event, over the island's future. Both the President and the Secretary of State felt a great distaste for Chiang Kai-shek who, they felt was largely responsible for the victory of the Chinese Communists the previous year. However, in this new situation, the government's position, Truman informed Congress, was that "the military neutralization of Formosa is without prejudice to political questions affecting that island. Our desire is that Formosa not become embroiled in hostilities disturbing to the peace of the Pacific and that all questions affecting Formosa be settled by peaceful means as envisaged in the Charter of the United Nations." [7]

The interjection of the Seventh Fleet brought heavy attack in the U.N. by the Soviet Union. The Russians circulated a petition charging the United States with aggression against Communist China in Formosa. To refute this charge Ambassador Austin cited the President's statements on the subject, that the order to the Seventh Fleet was an impartial neutralizing action "addressed both to the forces on Formosa and to those on the mainland."

It was while this U.N. debate was taking place that

---

[6] *Nippon Times,* August 2, 1950.
[7] Appendix PP, *Military Situation in the Far East,* p. 3383.

General MacArthur dispatched a letter to the Veterans of Foreign Wars, at their request, in which he emphasized the importance of retaining Formosa. "Nothing," he said, "could be more fallacious than the threadbare argument by those who advocate appeasement and defeatism in the Pacific that if we defend Formosa we alienate continental Asia." MacArthur's statement, reaching the press before it could be read at the VFW national encampment, was, like his Formosa visit interpreted as in conflict with President Truman's policy. The President directed the general to withdraw the statement and he did so, but international publicity had already been given the incident.

On August 28, in an effort to clarify America's policy, the President dispatched a lengthy letter to Ambassador Austin at the United Nations, reemphasizing the government's view that the United States would "welcome United Nations consideration of the case of Formosa. We would welcome full United Nations investigation here, or on the spot. We believe that United Nations consideration would contribute to a peaceful, rather than a forceable solution of that problem." [8] The President also forwarded this letter to MacArthur for his information.

With that, the issue temporarily rested.

Meanwhile, the war had been raging furiously around the Pusan perimeter as the North Korean army made desperate efforts to crack the iron ring. The U.N. lines continued to hold, and now MacArthur turned his attention to strategic planning to defeat the North Koreans. He conceived a brilliant plan, an amphibious assault behind enemy lines aimed at capturing Inchon and Seoul and cutting the enemy's communications south to the Pusan perimeter. To some Army officers this bold plan seemed

[8] *Ibid.*, p. 3476.

ill-advised. General J. Lawton Collins, the Army chief of staff, flew to Tokyo to try to talk MacArthur out of it. MacArthur, however, insisted on going ahead and both the Secretary of Defense and the President backed the supreme commander.

To carry out the operation MacArthur created the X Corps in Japan, composed of elements of the 1st Marine Division and the 7th United States Army division. A short period of intensive planning took place; studies were made of the tremendous Inchon tides; troops were briefed; supplies were piled up. On September 15, as the Eighth Army lashed out in a coordinated counteroffensive along the Naktong river line, the X Corps successfully stormed into Inchon. The Communists were caught by almost complete surprise. Although North Korean resistance stiffened as the Marines entered Seoul, the capital was swiftly recaptured. In the south Walker's offensive smashed through the North Korean lines.

Within two weeks of the Inchon landing, MacArthur's strategy had broken the back of the Communist armies and the North Koreans fled in confusion in an effort to escape the pincer closing upon them. Nearly all of the territory south of the 37th parallel was soon recaptured by the U.N. Command.[9] In the vicinity of the 38th parallel the Eighth Army and X Corps rested, while the applause of the Western world descended upon MacArthur. President Truman sent a message of congratulations.

On September 27 new instructions were sent to MacArthur. He was told that his military objective was the "destruction of the North Korean Armed Forces." The Joint Chiefs of Staff further cautioned him under no circumstances to cross the Manchurian or U.S.S.R. borders of

[9] Department of the Army, *Korea: 1950,* p. 150.

Korea. Operations against Manchuria or Russian territory were specifically to be avoided.

But meanwhile, Washington received several reports that the Chinese Communists were threatening to intervene in the war if United Nations troops crossed the 38th parallel into North Korea.[10] On October 1 Chou En-lai, the Chinese Communist premier, gave credence to the reports with a public pronouncement that China would "not allow seeing their neighbors being invaded by imperialists." [11] Several days later Chou announced flatly that China would send troops to defend North Korea.

The Chinese statements were troubling to the United States government, but it was felt there were good reasons for going ahead: the enemy could not be allowed to regroup and perhaps rebuild for a new attack. In addition, to the American government it seemed that a golden opportunity had presented itself to bring about the long-sought goal of a unified, independent Korea. There was also the distinct possibility that Peiping was bluffing.

Within the United Nations a widespread feeling that crossing the 38th parallel was necessary was also found.[12] On October 7, 1950, the U.N. General Assembly proceeded to adopt a resolution which recommended that "all appropriate steps be taken to ensure conditions of stability throughout Korea." The Assembly further established a new U.N. Commission "for the unification and rehabilitation of Korea."

On October 9, in a radio broadcast beamed to the North Koreans, MacArthur reported the U.N. action and called upon the Communists to surrender. There was no reply

[10] Acheson's testimony, *Military Situation in the Far East*, p. 1883.

[11] *Nippon Times*, October 2, 1950.

[12] However, the India Government, whose representative in Peiping had been warned of Chinese intervention plans, opposed entering North Korea.

and, on that day, the main body of the Eighth Army began the march into Communist territory, endeavoring to catch up with elements of the ROK Army which had crossed the 38th parallel on October 1.

The initial advances met little resistance and the situation seemed completely under control when, on October 14, MacArthur flew to Guam to meet a grateful President Truman. The mid-Pacific conference was initiated by the President, who had never met MacArthur and who wished a firsthand briefing on Far Eastern events, especially on possible Chinese or Russian intervention. The conference was brief but was, in the words of the President, "highly satisfactory." MacArthur, Truman, and the President's advisers discussed the entire Far Eastern situation, including the pending Japanese peace treaty. MacArthur gave his opinion that Chinese Communist or Russian intervention in Korea, or a combination of the two, was highly unlikely.

Following the conference, MacArthur enplaned immediately for Japan to turn his attention to the final phases of the war. On October 21 he commented briefly to newsmen that the Korean war "is very definitely coming to an end." [13] But, as quickly as he had turned defeat into victory, so the men of Peiping were to shatter his optimism.

[13] *Nippon Times*, October 21, 1950.

# 10

## Chinese Communist Intervention
## and the Military Stalemate

THE UNEXPECTED American reaction to the North Korean invasion must have been as troubling to Peiping as it was to Moscow—if only because it resulted in Truman's order to the Seventh Fleet neutralizing Formosa. In the weeks preceding the invasion, American intelligence learned that the Chinese Communists had increased their troop strength opposite Formosa from about 40,000 men to 156,000. In that same period, Radio Peiping broadcast repeated declarations of Communist intention of ending the Chinese civil war by "liberating Formosa" and destroying Chiang Kai-shek's forces. When the Seventh Fleet was interjected into the scene, the invasion of Formosa appeared imminent. Mao Tse-tung promptly denounced the American action, declaring that operations against Formosa would be carried out anyways "according to previous plans." [1] However, Mao was speaking in anger, for it was clear those plans were aborted.

Not only did this American action frustrate the Chinese Communists, but subsequent events in Korea probably gave them cause for alarm. As the remnants of the North Korean armies fled in confusion following MacArthur's brilliant stroke, the Chinese and Russians, we must surmise, went into hurried consultations, probably in accordance with the Soviet-Chinese Treaty negotiated in Mos-

[1] *Nippon Times,* June 30, 1950.

cow February 14, 1950, by Mao and Stalin. A key sentence of this treaty states that: "In the event of one of the High Contracting Parties being attacked by Japan or states allied with it, and thus being involved in a state of war, the other High Contracting Party will immediately render military and other assistance with all the means at its disposal." [2]

Although Japan was not involved, the Russians, facing a debacle of their plans in Korea, may have invoked this treaty of alliance, calling on their Chinese allies to aid the North Koreans. Where these Chinese-Russian negotiations took place and what concessions Stalin made to Mao remains veiled in Communist secrecy. But what is known is that Chinese troops began to move northward toward Manchuria and, in the last weeks of October 1950, they appeared in Korea in the guise of "volunteers."

These developments, of course, were hidden from the Americans, who continued their advance into North Korea to destroy the remnants of the North Korean forces. The Eighth Army, moving steadily northward, captured Pyongyang on October 19. At the same time, an airborne regimental combat team parachuted thirty miles beyond the Communist capital to close a trap on fleeing North Korean troops. On October 26 the X Corps, which had been withdrawn from the Seoul area, made an unopposed landing at the east coast port of Wonsan after that city had fallen to the ROK I Corps.

The Yalu river border was their last major objective when the U.N. forces came upon the first Chinese Communist "volunteers." On November 6, 1950, the United States government informed the U.N. Security Council of the presence of the Chinese in Korea. A chill ran through

---

[2] Appendix B, *Military Situation in the Far East*, p. 3172.

the collective back of the U.N.—with good reason, since the same day MacArthur was reporting to the Joint Chiefs that: "Men and material in large force are pouring across all bridges over the Yalu from Manchuria. This movement not only jeopardizes but threatens the ultimate destruction of the forces under my command." [3]

MacArthur had requested removal of restrictions on operations of his air power on the Manchurian border. Although the JCS was reluctant to permit air attacks which might cause Soviet or Chinese intervention, in view of MacArthur's message they authorized bombing at the frontier. However, the supreme commander was cautioned to be extremely careful to avoid violating Manchurian territory and air space. Within days the bridges across the Yalu, especially those at Sinuiju, came under attack by B-29s and carrier-based planes. [4]

Meanwhile, evidence continued to reach MacArthur's headquarters that the Chinese were intervening in force. On November 7, the general issued a special communique announcing that a new situation now faced the U.N. command. He said:

The Korean war was brought to a practical end with the closing of the trap on enemy elements north of Pyongyang and seizure of the East coastal area, resulting in raising the number of enemy prisoners of war in our hands to well over 135,-000 which with other losses amounting to over 200,000, brought casualties to 335,000, representing a fair estimate of North Korean total military strength. The defeat of the North Koreans and destruction of their armies was thereby decisive. In the face of this victory . . . the Communists committed one of the most offensive acts of international lawlessness . . . by moving without any notice of belligerency elements of alien Communist forces across the Yalu River into North Korea and

[3] General Collins' testimony, *Military Situation in the Far East*, p. 1233.
[4] *Nippon Times*, November 12, 13 and 15, 1950.

massing a great concentration of possible reinforcing divisions with adequate supply behind the privileged sanctuary of the adjacent Manchurian border.

A possible trap was thereby surreptitiously laid calculated to encompass the destruction of the United Nations forces engaged in restoring order and the processes of civil government in the North Korean border area. This potential danger was avoided . . . only by the timely detection and skillful maneuvering of the United Nations commander responsible for that sector, who with great perspicacity and skill completely reversed the movement of his forces in order to achieve the greater integration of tactical power necessitated by the new situation. . . . The present situation therefore is this. While the North Korean forces with which we were initially engaged have been destroyed or rendered impotent for military action, a new and fresh army now faces us backed up by a possibility of large alien reserves and adequate supply within easy reach of the enemy but beyond the limits of our present sphere of military action.

Whether and to what extent these reserves will be moved forward to reinforce units now committed remains to be seen and is a matter of the gravest international significance.[5]

The "privileged sanctuary" remained troubling to MacArthur and, in a message to the JCS, he complained of the restrictions. However, the only alternative was to give him authority to attack Manchurian bases, and this was contrary to the feelings of President Truman and his advisers "that we should not allow the action in Korea to extend into a general war. All-out military action against China had to be avoided, if for no other reason than because it was a gigantic booby trap."[6]

In the weeks which followed, a strange battlefield lull occurred as U.N. ground patrol units sought, and failed,

[5] *Ibid.*, November 7, 1950.
[6] Truman, *Years of Trial and Hope*, p. 378.

to make contact with the new enemy in any sizable force. Newspaper accounts began to speak of the "Chinese puzzle war." The puzzle was still unsolved when, on November 22, elements of the United States Seventh Division reached the Manchurian border on the west coast. The Chinese seemed to have disappeared from the scene.

But in reality, they had continued to pour across the Yalu, an army of 200,000 men which hid itself in the vicinity of the 40th parallel. It was a phantom army whose movement and concentration, according to S. L. A. Marshall, "had gone undetected. The enemy columns moved only by night, preserved an absolute camouflage discipline during their daylight rests and remained hidden to view under village rooftops after reaching the chosen ground. Air observation saw nothing of this mass maneuver. Civilian refugees brought no word of it. . . ." [7]

On November 24, 1950, MacArthur personally opened a hopeful "end-the-war" offensive. The U.N. commander was well aware that "new Red armies" were operating in the vicinity but he knew neither their strength nor their location. "We hoped," MacArthur said in justification later, "that the Army would be opposed by no more than a token Chinese force to support previous commitments but short of a full Chinese commitment to major operations." Now the awful weight of the hidden enemy fell upon the advancing Eighth Army and X Corps and, within hours, the initiative passed from the U.N. command. As advance units were overrun, the Eighth Army's forward movement stalled and tactical withdrawals began.

MacArthur ordered his field commanders to Tokyo for hurried consultations. On November 28, following these talks, he issued a special communiqué declaring that the

[7] S. L. A. Marshall, *The River and the Gauntlet* (New York: William Morrow & Co., 1953), p. 14.

entrance of Chinese continental armed forces into the conflict had created "an entirely new war." He concluded: "This situation, repugnant as it may be, poses issues beyond the authority of the United Nations military command—issues which must find their solution within the councils of the United Nations and chancelleries of the world." [8]

The next day MacArthur recommended to the Joint Chiefs that the United States now accept the Chinese Nationalist offer of 33,000 troops. After consultations with his advisers, Truman instructed the Joint Chiefs to call MacArthur's attention to the international implications of his recommendation. Great Britain, especially, would find it distasteful fighting alongside the Chinese Nationalists.

Several days later MacArthur reported to Washington that perhaps twenty-six Chinese divisions were in the line, and that unless he received great reinforcements, he would be forced into successive withdrawals or into beachhead positions. On December 3, the President approved an immediate reply to MacArthur: "We consider that the preservation of your forces is now the primary consideration. Consolidation of forces into beachheads is concurred in." [9]

To the Eighth Army and X Corps went orders to withdraw from North Korea. Within a few weeks the bulk of the Eighth Army made a successful withdrawal to the 38th parallel. In Northeast Korea the X Corps began an epic "advance to the rear" through the mountains to Hungnam on the east coast, where troops, supplies and equipment, and refugee Koreans, were evacuated by ship. In this manner, toward the close of December 1950, without a major battle, the Communist armies recovered North Korea.

[8] *Nippon Times*, November 29, 1950.
[9] Truman, *Years of Trial and Hope*, p. 393.

In the Western chancelleries the appearance of Chinese Communist armies in Korea invoked fears that a spreading Asian war would soon engulf the world. In a fortnight there dissipated the unity and determination which led to the defeat of the North Koreans. America's European allies greatly feared that if the United States now reacted violently to the Chinese intervention, it would, in Secretary Acheson's words, "incur grave risks of enlarging the war, and involving Europe in it, which would put them in a most exposed and dangerous position." The British felt the Americans "might gravely endanger the whole [North Atlantic] coalition, if we insisted on taking unilateral action which seemed to disregard their very grave dangers." [10]

How on edge the world was was seen by the reaction to the words "atom bomb" which the President used in a press conference on November 30. Truman replied to newsmen's questions that, if need be, in meeting the crisis, the United States would use every weapon in the American arsenal. This brought up the atom bomb and the President's questioners clearly inferred that this weapon might also be used. The news of Truman's statement resulted in great forebodings in Europe and a tense debate occurred in Britain's House of Commons. Afterwards, Prime Minister Clement Attlee announced to the cheers of the Parliament that he would fly to Washington for conferences with the President.

The second prime minister of Britain to travel to the United States to consult with the Americans on the conduct of a war, Attlee and his advisers arrived in the capital on December 4, 1950. The discussions between the two governments which followed ranged over all the problems facing the alliance in Europe, as well as Far Eastern prob-

[10] Acheson's testimony, *Military Situation in the Far East*, p. 1732.

lems and the Chinese intervention. The major divergence of opinion concerned Communist China, which Britain had recognized and which she believed to be far from a Kremlin satellite and possibly ripe for "Titoism." The Americans disagreed with this view. They also reaffirmed as American governmental policy the "MacArthur thesis" that the United States could not allow Formosa to fall into hostile hands. They further stated that they would not get out of Korea voluntarily. Attlee pledged Britain would continue to stand with the United States in Korea.

After three days of discussions, the Americans and British reached agreement that they would try to avoid a general war with China, and that they would hold on in Korea as long as possible. As for the atom bomb, Truman assured Attlee that he was not giving more active thought to using it.[11] Following the conferences, a public statement was issued in which the Anglo-American leaders declared they were ready to seek an end to the Korean hostilities by means of negotiations.

But it takes two parties to make a ceasefire, and the mood of the Chinese Communists was against an armistice except on their extraordinary terms. These terms, presented to the U.N. by General Wu Hsui-chuan, whom Peiping sent to Lake Success to press charges of aggression against the U.S., were: (1) the withdrawal of all foreign troops from Korea; (2) evacuation of United States personnel from Formosa; (3) ouster of the Chinese Nationalists from the U.N. and admission of the People's Republic of China; and (4) a voice in all Far Eastern affairs for the Peiping government.[12]

The U.N. General Assembly now entered the search for a ceasefire by creating a three-man committee to study the problem. This committee, composed of L. B. Pearson of

[11] Truman, *Years of Trial and Hope,* p. 410.
[12] *Nippon Times,* December 18, 1950.

Canada, Sir Benegal N. Rau of India, and Nasrollah Ente-
zam of Iran, consulted with the United States (as the unified
command) on its terms for a ceasefire. Now actively committed to ending the hostilities through negotiations, the American government agreed on eight points (i.e., establishment
of a demilitarized zone, supervision of a ceasefire by a United
Nations commission, prisoner-of-war exchange).

The U.N. committee presented the plan to General Wu.
At the same time, it cabled Peiping asking that Wu be instructed to remain in New York to discuss the matter. Chou
En-lai's reply, on December 22, 1950, was a rejection of the
committee's request. Chou repeated that, if the U.N. wished
a settlement, "all foreign troops must be withdrawn from
Korea, and Korea's domestic affairs must be settled by the
Korean people themselves. The American aggression forces
must be withdrawn from Taiwan. And the representatives
of the People's Republic of China must obtain a legitimate
status in the United Nations."[13]

In view of Peiping's stand, the three-man committee was
forced to report failure to the General Assembly. In a sup-
plementary report, the committee listed five principles for
seeking a peaceful settlement, including that a Big Four
meeting be convened with the Peiping government present
to discuss Far Eastern problems. Although these principles
went toward the Chinese Communist viewpoint, the United
States accepted them "as a basis for discussion." However,
on January 17, 1951, the Peiping government rejected the
five principles and reaffirmed its previous stand.

Military developments in Korea made it clear why the
Chinese Communists were so obdurate: they seemed capable of sweeping U.N. troops all the way back to the Pusan
perimeter. Although the Americans felt they could hold a

[13] Appendix PP, *Military Situation in the Far East,* p. 3513.

line in Korea, the Communists were exulting at the retreat of the "Anglo-American interventionists" and looking forward to the day "when the American aggressors will be totally defeated and annihilated. . . ." [14]

Meanwhile, fears arose over the safety of Japan, which had been stripped of American forces. On December 19 MacArthur requested reinforcements for the islands. But there were none available for either Japan or Korea: the American people were paying dearly for their great folly in destroying the marvelous armies they commanded at the end of World War II. The world's attention remained riveted on Korea, where hopes soon evaporated that the Chinese would be content with the recovery of the north. On December 25 Chinese Communist troops crossed the 38th parallel.

The leaders of the American government were vastly disturbed. As the possibility of a major military defeat arose, the Joint Chiefs of Staff, on December 29, requested MacArthur's views as to the conditions which might call for a decision to remain or evacuate Korea. MacArthur responded with four possible courses of action—all involving an expansion of the war against China. They were: (1) a blockade of the China coast; (2) naval and air bombardment of the Chinese industrial capacity to wage war; (3) use of Chinese Nationalist reinforcements; and (4) release of the Formosan garrison for diversionary actions on the Chinese mainland. The general, it was clear, wanted to fight.

But the American government did not. MacArthur's recommendations ran counter to the decision to try to avoid an expansion of the war and they were disapproved. On January 9, 1951, the Joint Chiefs informed MacArthur that retaliatory measures would not be permitted. He was directed to defend himself in successive positions, inflicting

[14] *Pravda*, January 5, 1951.

maximum damage to hostile forces in Korea subject to the primary consideration of the safety of his troops and his basic mission of protecting Japan. Should it become evident that evacuation was essential to avoid severe losses of men and material, he was at that time to withdraw from Korea to Japan.[15]

The supreme commander was severely disappointed by these instructions and what he considered to be fatal inactions in Washington. He dispatched another message, a particularly gloomy one, requesting clarification of his directives. He said that he could hold a beachhead in Korea but not without losses. He complained that his troops were "embittered by the shameful propaganda which has falsely condemned their fighting qualities and courage"; that unless the political basis on which "they are asked to trade life for time is clearly delineated, fully understood . . . their morale will become a serious threat to their efficiency." He said that, under the restrictions imposed on him, his position in Korea would eventually become untenable. Therefore, he recommended that, in the absence of overriding political considerations, "under these conditions the command should be withdrawn from the peninsula just as rapidly as it is feasible tactically to do so." He added that if overriding political considerations dictated that the United States hold a position in Korea, his command could do so "for any length of time up to its complete destruction." [16]

This pessimistic message brought Washington to its lowest point. There were new military consultations and, immediately after a new directive was prepared, two members of the Joint Chiefs of Staff—Generals Collins and Vandenberg—departed Washington for the Far East to see for themselves just what the situation was. The new JCS directive

15 Gen. Marshall's testimony, *Military Situation in the Far East*, p. 331.
16 Bradley's testimony, *Military Situation in the Far East*, p. 906.

to MacArthur, dated January 12, 1951, agreed that it was not feasible to hold in Korea for a protracted period. However, the Joint Chiefs pointed out it would be to the United States interest and to the interests of the U.N. "to gain some further time for essential military and diplomatic consultation with U.N. countries participating in [the] Korean effort" before evacuation was ordered. The JCS additionally said it was important that "maximum practical punishment be inflicted on Communist aggressors and that Korea not be evacuated unless actually forced by military considerations." [17]

President Truman also decided to send a personal letter to MacArthur to explain his views "as to our basic national and international purposes in continuing the resistance to aggression in Korea." The President, in this letter, outlined five points, including the key statement that he would have to give "constant thought to the main threat from the Soviet Union and to the need for a rapid expansion of our armed forces to meet this great danger." [18]

Several days later Collins and Vandenberg arrived in Tokyo and went into immediate consultation with MacArthur. Collins had brought with him a JCS study listing possible courses of action in the event an all-out war did develop with China. This study, which included sixteen suggested actions, incorporated MacArthur's recommendations. Collins left this study with the supreme commander.

The aura of military disaster still hovered in their minds when Collins and Vandenberg departed Japan for the peninsula. But once in Korea, they found a much improved situation. After visiting numerous front line units, they reported to Washington on January 17, 1951, that the Eighth Army was far from being a defeated command, that under

---

[17] *Ibid.*, pp. 737-738.
[18] Truman, *Years of Trial and Hope*, pp. 435-436.

the leadership of Lieutenant General Matthew B. Ridgway, General Walker's successor (Walker died in a jeep accident on December 23), the army was being revitalized. They said they had found high morale and self-confidence.

This good news was unexpected. It now appeared to the United States government that a military disaster was *not* in the making. The JCS study presented to MacArthur, which had outlined possible extreme American reactions, was abandoned. As confidence slowly returned, the United States moved to brand Communist China an aggressor and to initiate U.N. collective action against her. On January 30, 1951, the U.N. political committee adopted a United States resolution on the matter and called for a study of economic sanctions. The General Assembly acted favorably on February 1 when, by a vote of forty-four to seven, it declared Communist China an aggressor in Korea.

The renewed confidence in the Eighth Army was well placed. Under Ridgway's command, the army began planning for its first offensive action since the northern retreat. These preparations had neared completion when the Chinese Communists began what Peiping apparently hoped would be the final assault on the U.N. forces. But the Chinese ran into determined resistance from the Eighth Army and suffered huge losses. On February 20, Ridgway announced that the Communist offensive had been halted. Now it was the Eighth Army's turn and it began a march northward. On March 15 Seoul was recaptured from the Communists for the second and last time. A few weeks later South Korean troops recrossed the 38th parallel as the offensive continued. On April 3 troops of the American 1st Cavalry Division also recrossed the parallel into North Korea.

The entire complexion of the war had changed once more.

While these military advances took place, a series of incidents occurred on the political scene which led to the dramatic ouster of General MacArthur from all his commands. MacArthur's recall from the Far East by the President was extremely important in that it clearly and definitely established the policies which the United States government was embarked upon in Korea.

The brilliant military commander had, for a number of years, been something more than an army officer. Because of his high rank, he found himself often entering political fields, especially in his position as supreme commander over occupation forces in Japan, where he proclaimed and expounded on great civil issues affecting Japan's "democratization." MacArthur was sought after by his many admirers to give his views on various aspects of the cold war. So it was no surprise when, in response to a Veterans of Foreign Wars request, he entered into the Formosa discussion in August 1950.[19]

Later, after the Chinese Communist intervention, MacArthur repeatedly, in his communiques to Washington, called for new political decisions to meet the crisis. His views continued to be solicited by newspapermen and American press media, stirring such controversy that, on December 6, 1950, he was requested by the Joint Chiefs to exercise "extreme caution in public statements" and to refrain "from direct communication on military or foreign policy with newspapers, magazines or other publicity media in the United States."[20]

In March 1951, after the Eighth Army had demonstrated the weaknesses of the Chinese Communist armies, the Truman administration felt the time was appropriate to seek anew discussions for a settlement in Korea. MacArthur was

[19] See Chapter 9, p. 118.
[20] Appendix PP, *Military Situation in the Far East*, pp. 3536 and 3542.

informed of State Department planning, which involved consultations with U.N. members who had contributed forces to the Korean campaign.. Under the American plan, the President was to issue a declaration that, since the aggressors had been driven back into North Korea and the original aggression repelled, the U.N. was prepared to enter into arrangements to conclude the fighting and obtain a prompt settlement.

However, on March 24 MacArthur issued a statement in Tokyo in which he pointed out the general weaknesses that had been uncovered by Chinese losses in recent battles. He stated that Red China lacked the industrial capacity to conduct modern war; that her numerical superiority was overcome by existing methods of mass destruction; and that it had been shown that Red China could not by force of arms conquer Korea. "The enemy, therefore," MacArthur said, "must by now be painfully aware that a decision of the United Nations to depart from its tolerant effort to contain the war to the area of Korea, through an expansion of our military operations to its coastal areas and interior bases, would doom Red China to the risk of imminent military collapse." MacArthur thereupon offered to meet with the enemy commander in the field to realize the political objectives of the U.N. in Korea.[21]

When word of MacArthur's statement reached Washington, there was consternation. His statement clearly was at cross purposes with the American diplomatic efforts in the U.N. to end the fighting; his threat seemed to imply a new United States plan of action against China. Inquiries from America's allies soon began arriving at the State Department. "Deeply shocked," the President ordered a message sent to MacArthur that same day, March 24, referring him

[21] Truman, *Years of Trial and Hope,* pp. 440-441.

to the JCS message of December 6 about making public statements on military or foreign policy.

This latest telegram to MacArthur arrived, however, after he had responded to a letter to Joseph W. Martin, Republican leader in Congress. In this letter, dated March 20, MacArthur called for meeting "force with maximum counterforce as we have never failed to do in the past." He also reiterated his views concerning use of Chinese Nationalist forces on Formosa. Congressman Martin, well aware of the divergence of opinion that had developed between Washington and Tokyo, released MacArthur's letter to the press on April 6. Five days later President Truman relieved the general of all his commands. Ridgway was named Far East and U.N. commander and General James Van Fleet was sent to Korea to take over the Eighth Army.

A great public furor, encouraged by Republican opponents of the administration, followed MacArthur's firing. In a dramatic return to the United States and appearance before a joint meeting of Congress on April 19, 1951, MacArthur recalled the four recommendations he had made in December, 1950, calling for drastic action against China. He said:

For entertaining these views all professionally designed to support our forces committed to Korea and bring hostilities to an end and with the least possible delay and at a saving of countless American and Allied lives, I have been severely criticized in lay circles, principally abroad, despite my understanding that from a military standpoint the above views have been fully shared in the past by practically every military leader concerned with the Korean campaign, including our own Joint Chiefs of Staff. [Here MacArthur referred to the JCS study of January, 1951, on possible courses of action in event of all-out war with China.]

I called for reinforcements, but was informed that reinforce-

ments were not available. I made clear that if not permitted
to utilize the friendly Chinese force of some 600,000 men on
Formosa; if not permitted to blockade the China coast to
prevent the Chinese Reds from getting succor from without;
and if there were to be no hope of major reinforcements, the
position of the command from the military standpoint for-
bade victory. We could hold in Korea by constant maneuver
and at an approximate area where our supply advantages
were in balance with the supply line disadvantages of the
enemy, but we could hope at best for only an indecisive campaign, with its terrible and constant attrition upon our forces
if the enemy utilized his full military potential. I have constantly called for the new political decisions essential to a
solution. . . .[22]

Several weeks after MacArthur's address to Congress,
there began the strange spectacle of a congressional inquiry
into MacArthur's recall and the conduct of the war while
it still raged. The Senators first heard MacArthur defend
and explain his position, and then heard and crossexamined
members of the administration, including Secretary of Defense Marshall, Generals Bradley, Collins, and Vandenberg, Admiral Sherman, Acheson, and former Secretary of
Defense Johnson. The administration's position was de-
fended unanimously by the Joint Chiefs of Staff and the
Secretaries of State and Defense. Secretary Marshall summed
up the government's stand in his opening remark before
the Senate committee:

Our position in Korea [he said], continues to be the defeat of
the aggression and the restoration of peace. We have persist-
ently sought to confine the conflict to Korea and to prevent
its spreading into a third World War. In this effort, we stand
allied with the great majority of our fellow members of the
United Nations. Our efforts have succeeded in thwarting the

[22] Appendix PP, *Military Situation in the Far East*, pp. 3553-58.

aggressors in Korea, and in stemming the tide of aggression in Southwest Asia and elsewhere throughout the world. Our efforts in Korea have given us some sorely needed time and impetus to accelerate the building of our defenses and those of our allies against the threatened onslaught of Soviet imperialism.

General MacArthur, on the other hand, would have us, on our own initiative, carry the conflict beyond Korea against the mainland of China, both from the sea and from the air. He would have us accept the risk of involvement not only in an extension of the war with Red China, but in an all-out war with the Soviet Union. He would have us do this even at the expense of losing our allies and wrecking the coalition of free peoples throughout the world. He would have us do this even though the effort of such action might expose Western Europe to attack by the millions of Soviet troops poised in Middle and Eastern Europe.

This fundamental divergence . . . arises from the inherent difference between the position of the field commander, whose mission is limited to a particular area . . . and the position of the Joint Chiefs of Staff, the Secretary of Defense and the President, who are responsible for the total security of the United States. . . .[23]

While the MacArthur furor held the world's attention, the Chinese Communist armies in Korea began their second spring offensive in April 1951. Although they succeeded in forcing the Eighth Army to retire eighteen to twenty miles, by May 1 this offensive was also halted, with the Chinese again sustaining heavy losses. A third Communist effort several weeks later produced additional thousands of Chinese dead.

Severely punished and unable to advance in face of the fire-power of the Eighth Army, the Chinese armies began to retire to the north. The American and U.N. force fol-

[23] Marshall's testimony, *Military Situation in the Far East*, pp. 324-325.

lowed closely and, on May 24, crossed the 38th parallel in force. The Chinese began counter-attacking fiercely in an effort to halt the Eighth Army's drive in the Chorwon-Kumwha-Pyonggang triangle north of the parallel.

By June 1951—almost a year from the day of the original Communist assault—the myth of the Chinese Communist hordes sweeping the United Nations off the peninsula had been decisively punctured. But also ended was the hope that Korea could be united by force. Both sides had tried, and both had failed.

# 11

## The Frustrating
## Armistice Negotiations

THE AMERICAN government, as we have seen, had made it exceedingly clear that it had no intention of pushing to the Yalu river, that it would accept an honorable truce. But the decision as to whether there would be a ceasefire was not to be made in Washington. Peiping and Moscow would decide, as they had decided the initial aggression.

Significantly, it was only after the Communist armies had failed to conquer South Korea, after the casualties to Mao's best troops climbed ever higher, that the desire for a ceasefire was indicated by the Communist rulers. Thus in June 1951—with the Russians' colossal error in starting the Korean conflict having been erased through the efforts of the Chinese Communists—the Soviet Union made a formal bid to end the fighting. The Russian proposal for a ceasefire was made on June 23, in an address to the United Nations by the Soviet delegate, Jacob Malik. He said:

"The Soviet peoples believe that as a first step, discussions should be started between the belligerents for a ceasefire and an armistice providing for the mutual withdrawal of forces from the 38th parallel." [1]

This was what Washington had been waiting for. A week after the Malik speech, General Ridgway, the U.N. commander, broadcast a statement to the Communist command-

[1] U.S. Congress, Senate, *The United States and the Korean Problem*, p. 57.

ers, Generals Kim Il Sung and Peng Teh-huai, that he had
"been informed that you may wish a meeting to discuss an
armistice providing for the cessation of hostilities and all
acts of armed force in Korea." The Communists replied on
July 1, acknowledging that they "had been authorized to
inform you that we agree to meet your representative for
conducting talks." They suggested the two parties meet in
the area of Kaesong on the 38th parallel. General Ridgway
accepted this suggestion. Liaison officers of both sides met a
week later and, on July 10, 1951, the first conference of the
full armistice delegations was convened.

This first session was followed by hundreds more between
the two military commands, meetings which were to be
dragged out for almost two years. They were full of acri-
mony, bitterness, and hatred. The Communists appeared to
be in no hurry to come to an agreement and, while they
procrastinated, the two opposing armies fought bloody duels
in the hills and mountains of central Korea.

The U.N. command's armistice delegation was headed by
Vice Admiral C. Turner Joy.* His opposite number on the
Communist side was General Nam Il, a Soviet citizen of
Korean descent.[2]

At the first meeting on July 10, the first disagreement
arose. The Americans proposed that twenty Western newsmen be allowed to cover the armistice conference; the Communists objected to the plan. After a short recess, Admiral
Joy returned to the conference table with a statement from
General Ridgway, stating that the presence of the newsmen
at a conference "of such major importance to the entire

* In future references to the U.N. delegation, the author will refer to
it as the U.S. delegation, since the Americans constituted the major
component and were made responsible for the negotiations.

[2] Nam Il, according to the Pentagon, served in the Soviet Army in
World War II.

world is considered an inherent right by members of the United Nations." [3] Joy further told the Communists his delegation would recess until such time as they agreed to the presence of the newsmen. The delay which followed, while the Communist delegation sought instructions, was to be repeated many times. On July 14, the Communist directive was received and Nam Il informed Joy that the news coverage would be allowed.

The next problem facing the conference was to reach agreement on an agenda. The Communists at once tried to prejudice matters in their favor by using language which would recognize the 38th parallel as the demarcation line (the Eighth Army was north of the parallel). The Americans rejected this. Then the Communists proposed an agenda item calling for the withdrawal of foreign troops from Korea. This also was rejected, with Secretary of Defense Marshall in Washington defining what Ridgway was trying to accomplish ". . . the negotiation of a suitable military armistice. This negotiation on the battlefield is an entirely different problem from the negotiation of a political settlement. If an acceptable armistice can be obtained, discussion of the political questions can follow on the highest governmental level." [4]

Agreement on the agenda was finally reached on July 26, 1951, as follows:

1. Adoption of an agenda.
2. Fixing a military demarcation line between both sides so as to establish a demilitarized zone as a basic condition for a ceasefire.

[3] General Headquarters, UNC (Advance), *Transcript of Proceedings, Second Session, Conference at Kaesong, Korea, on Armistice Proposal,* July 10, 1951, p. 23.
[4] U.S. Congress, Senate, *The United States and the Korean Problem,* p. 58.

3. Concrete arrangements for the realization of a cease-fire and an armistice, including the composition, authority, and functions of a supervising organization.

4. Arrangements relating to prisoners of war (POWs).

5. Recommendations to the governments of the countries concerned on both sides.

The conference immediately proceeded to Item 2 on the agenda, since Item 1 was already adopted. Item 2 proved a pitfall. With the Eighth Army well in control of territory north of the 38th parallel, the Americans took the position that the final demarcation line should be related to the "line of contact" of opposing forces and the "military realities" of the situation. Nam Il denounced this plan as "unworthy." On the other hand, he proposed fixing the 38th parallel as the demarcation line, since "it clearly reflected," he said, "the relative war power of both sides at the present stage."[5]

The Americans were determined they would not give up the territory in North Korea they had won through force of arms. A hard and fast deadlock ensued as futile meeting followed futile meeting. Complained the chairman of the presidium of the North Korean regime in *Pravda*: "The line of military demarcation proposed by the Americans would cut an area of more than 13,000 square kilometers off the southern part of our republic. . . . This line would pass in the rear of our present position. . . . The Korean people have not agreed to the negotiations in Kaesong in order to make a deal with the American usurpers over their own territory. . . ."[6] At the August 22 meeting, Nam Il arose to charge that U.N. warplanes had "violated" the air of Kaesong, thereby creating an atmosphere menacing to the conference. Because of this, the Communist general declared, the armis-

---

[5] General Headquarters, UNC (Advance), *Transcript of Proceedings, Twelfth Session*, July 28, 1951, p. 5.

[6] *Pravda*, August 15, 1951.

tice negotiations were "off from now on." The Communists thereupon walked out.

The Americans investigated the charge and concluded that it was false. Some felt, in seeking the true reasons for the Communist break-off of negotiations, the answer could be found in the United States-sponsored peace treaty with Japan. In late August and early September 1951, the United States prepared the way for the signing in San Francisco of the treaty ending the state of war between Japan and the allies. The Soviet Union opposed the treaty and refused to sign or recognize it. The Communists' comments in *Pravda* tied in the Japanese treaty with Kaesong but in reverse. Said *Pravda:*

Even the casual observer must have noticed that as the opening date of the San Francisco Conference approached, the provocative American violations of the Kaesong neutral zone became increasingly regular and far reaching. The San Francisco Conference was convened to the accompaniment of the bombs being dropped by the American planes upon the Kaesong neutral zone, as well as to the accompaniment of hysterical squeals from the venal American press at the disruption of the Kaesong negotiations. This "background" was essential for U.S. ruling circles so that they could exert pressure upon those participants at the San Francisco production. . . .[7]

In any event, the Kaesong negotiations remained suspended for two months. During that time the Communists repeated their charge that the conference site had been violated by U.N. planes. In an effort to overcome this Communist obstruction and to allow the Communists to make a face-saving withdrawal, and thus proceed with the negotiations, General Ridgway on September 27 offered to meet with the Communists at a new site, approximately midway between the battle lines. After some further procrastination,

[7] *Ibid.,* September 18, 1951.

the Communists finally accepted Ridgway's suggestion. They proposed the site of Panmunjom. On October 21, 1951, an agreement was signed for resumption of the negotiations. Three days later the full armistice conference reconvened.

On October 27 Nam Il, to the surprise of the United States delegates, agreed to the "line of contact" plan for the demarcation line. Item 2 on the agenda was turned over to staff officers who were to draw the battle line across Korea.

Between November 1951, and the spring of 1952, steady, if nerve-racking, progress was made in the negotiations. The numerous subcommittees of the two delegations resolved the problem of how to implement the ceasefire (through organization of a Military Armistice Commission aided by Joint Observer Teams). Agreement was reached on creation of a Neutral Nations Supervisory Commission to "supervise, observe, inspect and investigate adherence to the terms of the armistice agreement relative to the introduction into Korea of reinforcing military personnel and equipment."

However, all progress appeared to have been in vain when the armistice conference got around to Item 4 on the agenda —arrangements relating to POWs. On the subject of war prisoners, the worst, the most troublesome, and eventually the most bloody deadlock of all occurred.

The trouble over the prisoners began in December 1951, when both sides agreed to exchange lists of personnel they had captured. The United Nations list, as presented to the Communists, contained the names of 132,474 Chinese and North Koreans.[8] The Communist list contained 11,559

[8] The Americans later reclassified 11,000 of the prisoners they held as civilians and these persons were released. The Communist list did not include an estimated 65,000 South Koreans captured by them who were "re-educated" and "released at the front."

names, including the name of General Dean, which was the first official word that he was alive.

In approaching the problem of the release of the war prisoners, the U.N. command took the position that prisoners should not be forced to return to the Communist side. Many of the prisoners captured by U.N. units stated they would violently resist repatriation, that they feared death or injury if they did return. The Communist position, however, was that *all* Chinese and North Korean soldiers in the U.N. custody must be repatriated. Admiral Joy, in an effort to win an agreement, suggested to the Communists in April 1952, that the negotiations temporarily go into secret session so that both sides could discuss the problem freely away from the glare of world publicity. Nam Il agreed to this procedure.

In the closed meetings which followed, Nam Il asked the Americans for a round number estimate of the prisoners they would be able to repatriate. Joy responded that this could only be determined by interviewing the individual prisoners. At this point, the Americans assumed that only a relatively small percentage of the POWs in their detention camps would violently resist repatriation. Thus Admiral Joy suggested to Nam Il that the Communist command issue an amnesty statement to the prisoners, promising no punishment to them, to be followed by the interviews to determine which persons would choose freely to return. The Communists agreed to this procedure and prepared an amnesty statement which was distributed to all prisoners under U.N. control. Then the interviewing began.

The Americans were somewhat startled by the results: of 106,000 prisoners who consented to be interviewed, only 70,000 said they desired to return north. Completion of the interviewing program brought the total of those who could be repatriated without force to 83,000 (including 76,600

North Koreans and 6400 Chinese). When these figures were presented to the Communist side, a disbelieving Nam Il promptly branded the interviews as "illegal" and he again demanded that all prisoners must be repatriated. The problem seemed impossible of solution.

Washington now gave Ridgway and Joy permission to indulge in some horse-trading over some other unsettled issues in an effort to break the POW deadlock. These issues were: (1) restrictions on the rehabilitation and construction of airfields following a ceasefire; and (2) the makeup of the Neutral Nations Supervisory Commission. On April 28, 1952, Joy offered the Communist side the following compromise proposal:

a. There be no forced repatriation of prisoners.

b. The U.N. Command would not insist on prohibiting reconstruction and rehabilitation of airfields.

c. The U.N. Command would agree to Poland and Czechoslovakia as members of the Commission, if the Communists agreed to Sweden and Switzerland. (This would drop the Communist suggestion of Soviet Russia as a neutral member.) [9]

Nam Il asked for a three-day recess while his side considered this plan. On reconvening the conference May 2, 1952, Nam Il presented the Communist answer. He said his side would accept the American position on the Supervisory Commission (i.e., dropping the Soviet Union), but that the U.N. Command must agree to no restrictions on airfield facilities and, as previously demanded, agree to return all captured personnel.

The Americans refused this trade, once more stating that they would not forcibly repatriate any prisoner.

[9] Headquarters UNC (Advance), *Record of Events, Forty-fourth Session, 18th Meeting at Panmunjom, Military Armistice Conference,* April 28, 1952, pp. 2-4.

It was at this point in the deadlocked conference that there occurred a series of amazing and bloody prisoner riots in the U.N. command's prisoner enclosures. Fervent Communist prisoners in compounds on Koje and Cheju islands increased their agitation as the prisoner exchange issue reached the delicate stage at Panmunjom. Their incitement of the prisoners reached a peak on May 7, 1952, when Brigadier General Francis T. Dodd, the American commander on Koje, was seized and dragged into one of the compounds.

The seizure of Dodd occurred just as a change in command was taking place in Tokyo: Ridgway was turning over his command to General Mark W. Clark and proceeding to NATO in Europe. In one of his last orders, Ridgway promptly directed Eighth Army commander Van Fleet to appoint a successor to Dodd and to take all necessary measures to release the captured commander. Van Fleet dispatched Brigadier General Charles F. Colson to be new POW commander. Additional troops and tanks were also sent. Colson, after much embarrassing negotiations with the Communist prisoners, finally obtained Dodd's release on May 12, 1952.

At Panmunjom Nam Il was feeling his strength. He denounced the activities of the Americans in suppressing the prisoner riots. It was "mass massacre," he said, an attempt "to coerce our captured personnel in acceptance of your forcible retention. The unswerving will of our captured personnel to return to their homes has been fully demonstrated." [10] The Communist press also denounced the Americans who, cried *Pravda*, had "given themselves to Hitlerite tyranny and bloody terrorism." [11]

In succeeding months data obtained from the Communist prisoners shed additional light on the riots, indicating that

[10] *Ibid.*
[11] *Pravda*, May 19, 24, 1952.

specific orders had been received by the POWs from the Communist high command, to capture American officers if possible, to riot and spill blood if necessary, so as to demonstrate their "unswerving will" to return to the north.[12] But if the Communists had really hoped that the riots would force the United States to give up the principle of no forced repatriation, they were quickly disillusioned. Although smarting under Nam Il's caustic attacks, the American delegation refused to budge from its stand.

The Joint Chiefs of Staff, with Ridgway's departure, also authorized the relief of Admiral Joy as senior delegate to the conference. The admiral, in his final meeting with Nam Il on May 22, issued a lengthy statement summing up the long search for a ceasefire. He once again emphasized to Nam Il that the United Nations would not secede from its position on war prisoners. "After ten months and twelve days," Joy said, "I feel there is nothing more for me to do. There is nothing left to negotiate."[13]

Joy's successor, Major General William K. Harrison, in succeeding and similarly fruitless meetings with the Communists, also reiterated that the United Nations Command "will not drive personnel to you at the point of a bayonet."[14]

[12] Mark W. Clark, *From the Danube to the Yalu* (New York: Harpers & Brothers, 1954), p. 36.
[13] Headquarters UNC (Advance), *Transcript of Proceedings, Sixty-fifth Session, 39th Meeting at Panmunjom, Military Armistice Conference,* May 22, 1952, p. 3.
[14] *Ibid., Seventy-fourth Session,* June 3, 1952, p. 3.

# 12

## The Communists Give In

GENERAL MARK CLARK, the third United Nations commander, found that in his new assignment he faced a double deadlock—on the battlefield and at the conference table. Examining the battlefield deadlock, Clark began in June 1952 to explore new ways and means of punishing the Communist forces. "Since it was not our government's policy to seek a military decision," he later wrote in *From the Danube to the Yalu*, "the next best thing was to make the stalemate more expensive for the Communists than for us, to hit them where it hurt, to worry them, to convince them by force that the price tag on an armistice was going up, not down." [1]

Out of this review came the decision, approved by the government, to expand air assaults on targets in North Korea, including the important Suiho dam on the Yalu, the largest hydroelectric installation in the Far East. The destruction of this dam, on June 23, 1952, was a national calamity for the North Koreans, destroying their major source of power.

Clark also recommended to Washington the buildup of the Republic of Korea army into a larger and more effective fighting force. In addition, like his predecessors, he recommended that Chinese Nationalist troops be used against the Chinese Communists in Korea.

Of these recommendations, the government delayed action on the buildup of the South Korean army until the subject was injected into the 1952 national election cam-

[1] Clark, *op. cit.*, p. 69.

paign, and did not respond on the proposal to use the Chinese Nationalists.

After reviewing the frustrating armistice negotiations Clark, early in June 1952, asked Washington's permission to recess the talks for three-day periods—whether the Communists agreed to do so or not. This authority was granted. The first recess was called unilaterally by General Harrison on June 7 and confused and surprised the Communists. The Americans were pleased and thereafter, three- and four-day U.N. Command walkouts became the rule. Soon the initiative at the conference table, which was lost during the Koje riots, returned to the Americans.

However, the deadlock over the prisoner issue continued unbroken. In their search for a solution, the Americans developed three alternate plans and offered these to the Communists on September 28. One of these proposals called for turning over the nonrepatriate POWs to representatives of a mutually-agreed upon country, which would interview them and afterward allow them to go to the side of their choice.[2] All three plans embodied the idea of no forced repatriation.

While the Communists were considering these plans, General Clark requested and received Washington's approval to recess the conference if it was clear no progress was being made. After a ten-day adjournment, the Communists returned to Panmunjom with their answer to the U.N. Command's three proposals—a rejection. They repeated their argument for "total repatriation." After hearing the Communists' rejection, General Harrison informed Nam Il that he was thereby recessing the truce meetings indefinitely. He said:

[2] Headquarters UNC (Advance), *One hundred twenty-first Session, 95th Meeting at Panmunjom, Military Armistice Conference*, September 28, 1952, pp. 2-4.

We are not terminating these armistice negotiations, we are merely recessing them. We are willing to meet with you at any time that you are ready to accept one of our proposals or to make a constructive proposal of your own, in writing, which could lead to an honorable armistice. . . . Since you have offered nothing constructive, we stand in recess.[3]

The United States delegation arose and walked from the building.

The Communists gave every indication of being upset by this action. During the weeks that followed, a note of anxiety crept into their radio attacks on the Americans. General Clark dispatched a letter to Kim Il Sung and Peng Teh-huai, restating his position, that he was ready and willing to meet again with the Communist delegation "as soon as you indicate willingness to negotiate in good faith. . . ." [4]

There was still another place in which Clark tried to seize the initiative—in the bunker-marked hills and pitted valleys of central Korea.

Van Fleet and his subordinate commanders [Clark wrote], chafed under the conditions of this defensive war, as did I, and he occasionally submitted plans for limited offensives in narrow sectors. Except in rare instances I rejected them. There was no point in losing men if we weren't going whole hog. One exception was the Sniper's Ridge-Triangle Hill operation that began on October 14, 1952, just six days after Harrison recessed the armistice talks. . . .[5]

This offensive initiated some of the heaviest fighting in a year, a "grim, face-saving slugging match" that led to heavy casualties on both sides, with little profit for either. Clark considered the operation unsuccessful.[6]

[3] *Ibid., One hundred twenty-second Session,* October 8, 1952, p. 9.
[4] Headquarters UNC (Advance), *62d Supplement,* October 19-25, 1952, pp. 1-2.
[5] Clark, *op. cit.,* p. 78.
[6] *Ibid.,* p. 79.

The flare-up of heavy fighting occurred at a time when
the United States was in the final weeks of the 1952 presidential election campaign. The war had become extremely
unpopular with the American people and the Republican
candidate, General Dwight D. Eisenhower, made it an important campaign issue. In one of his final speeches before
the election, he promised that, if elected, he would visit
Korea to seek a way to end the war. Following his landslide
victory, the President-elect prepared to fly to Korea.

General Clark was notified of Eisenhower's impending
visit, but he had received no instructions from the Joint
Chiefs on what his former commander in Europe might
wish to discuss. He therefore prepared a list of subjects he
thought would interest Eisenhower, including detailed information on the forces and plans required to win a military victory in Korea "should the new administration decide
to take such a course." However, after meeting and talking
with Eisenhower, Clark learned that the President-elect was
committed to seeking an honorable truce.[7]

After visiting the battle lines, Eisenhower, in a statement
to the press before his departure from Korea, indicated he
would try to avoid an enlargement of the war. "How difficult it seems to be in a war of this kind," he said, "to work
out a plan that would bring a positive and definite victory
without possibly running grave risks of enlarging the war." [8]
Later, following his inauguration, the new President addressed a joint session of the Congress on February 2, 1953,
and spoke of the painful war in Korea. But he gave no
concrete plan except to announce that increased attention
would be given to the growth of the ROK armed forces and

[7] *Ibid.*, p. 233.
[8] *U.S. Army Combat Forces Journal,* January 1953, p. 5.

also that "the Seventh Fleet no longer [would] be employed to shield Communist China." [9]

The election to the American Presidency of the man who launched the successful amphibious assault on Nazi Gerfany's "Fortress Europe" undoubtedly was not reassuring to Moscow or Peiping. It may have been a factor which impinged upon events to bring the war to a close. But there were other factors. One of these, whose importance it is difficult to overestimate, was the death of Premier Stalin on March 5, 1953. Stalin's error in approving the Korean invasion must have become apparent to many in the Kremlin, but while he lived an error by the "infallible" leader could not be admitted.

Still another important factor was the persistent activity of the Government of India in attempting to bring about the longed-for armistice. The Indians initiated certain actions which later helped the combatants. One of these was a resolution introduced into the U.N. General Assembly on December 3, 1952, calling for a ceasefire on the basis that "force shall not be used" against the POWs but that there be organized a repatriation commission composed of Czechoslovakia, Poland, Sweden, and Switzerland, to take charge of the prisoners for 120 days. During that period, the Indians proposed, the prisoners would have their rights explained to them and then would choose freely where they would go. The Indian plan was accepted by fifty-four nations, but was initially rejected by Moscow and Peiping.

A few days later, another Indian resolution, presented to the League of Red Cross Societies at Geneva, Switzerland, eventually became the vehicle which led to the ceasefire. In this second resolution, the Indians recommended that sick

[9] U.S. Congress, Senate, *The United States and the Korean Problem*, pp. 76-77.

and wounded prisoners be exchanged in advance of a cease-fire. The resolution was approved by the League.

Although nothing resulted immediately from this pro-posal, the JCS on February 19, 1953, advised Clark that a similar resolution might be introduced into the General Assembly. The JCS reported that the State Department had suggested that the U.N. commander "pick up the ball in advance and put the proposition of exchanging sick and wounded POW's directly to the Communist command-ers." [10] General Clark promptly followed up. On February 22, in a letter to Kim Il Sung and Peng Teh-huai, he stated he was ready immediately to repatriate the seriously sick and wounded prisoners, if the Communists would agree to do the same. For more than a month there was silence from the Communist side. In that month Stalin died. Thirteen days after his death, the Communists for-warded their reply—agreeing to the exchange of sick and wounded. The Communists further stated:

At the same time we consider that the reasonable settlement of the question of exchanging sick and injured prisoners of war of both sides during the period of hostilities should be made to lead to the smooth settlement of the entire question of prisoners of war, thereby achieving an armistice in Korea for which people throughout the world are longing. There-fore our side proposes that the Delegates for armistice nego-tiations of both sides immediately resume the negotiations of Panmunjom.[11]

This was an unexpected dividend and Clark promptly suggested to the Communists a meeting of liaison officers to make arrangements for the prisoner exchange. As a sec-ond order of business, the U.N. commander suggested they

[10] Clark, *op. cit.*, p. 240.
[11] Headquarters UNC (Advance), *84th Supplement*, March 29, April 4, 1953, pp. 2-8.

should then arrange for a resumption of the armistice negotiations.

On March 30 Chou En-lai issued a public statement on
the matter, approving the exchange of sick and wounded
prisoners, and again stating that:

"Both parties to the negotiations should undertake to
repatriate immediately after the cessation of hostilities all
those prisoners of war in their custody who insist on repatriation, and to hand over the remaining prisoners of
war to a neutral state so as to ensure a just solution to the
question of their repatriation." This did not mean, Chou
said, that Peiping acknowledged that there were prisoners
"who allegedly refuse repatriation." He was confident that
proper explanations would convince all prisoners to return home.[12] Chou's statement was seconded by the North
Koreans.

The log jam had finally broken. When the liaison officers met once more on April 6, 1953, agreements were
reached with comparative ease. On April 11 a formal agreement was signed for exchanging the sick and wounded
POWs. The operation, known as "Little Switch," began
on April 20. In the weeks that followed the U.N. command
turned over 6670 sick and injured Chinese and North Korean prisoners. In return, the Communists surrendered
684 United Nations personnel, including 149 Americans.

The successful realization of "Little Switch," although
accompanied by Communist bad faith in withholding some
seriously ill U.N. personnel, sent American hopes soaring.
On April 26, the first plenary session of the reconvened
armistice conference was held and the delegates plunged
into the task of resolving their last bits of disagreement.
The composition of the Neutral Nations Supervisory Commission was agreed to, and agreement was also reached on

[12] *Ibid.*

India as the neutral state to take charge of the nonrepatriate prisoners—dependent on the Indians' agreeing to accept the role.

But even as this progress was recorded towards the longed-for goal, there loomed the figure of a man much ignored. Syngman Rhee, president of the Republic of Korea, strode upon the stage, threatening to wreck any armistice that might be signed.

# 13

## Rhee's Rebellion

THE TRUE tragedy of Korea was that so often its destiny had been determined by others. The people of Korea, that miserable party most affected by the international rivalries which swept across their homeland, had had little to say about their future. The situation left them, and their leaders in South Korea, bitter, frustrated, and indignant. Finally, in the spring of 1953, Syngman Rhee tried to grasp the reins of his nation's destiny.

The fact that Rhee was strongly opposed to an armistice which left his country divided was well known to his American allies. Rhee's opposition had begun almost from the moment that the Soviet Union finally agreed to talk about an armistice. The day after Malik made his proposal on June 23, 1951, Rhee issued a statement denouncing any end to the war which did not extend his republic's boundaries to the natural front on the Yalu and Tumen rivers. He said: "If we settle for anything less than the security and integrity of this country, we will have betrayed the trust of those who in the fight for freedom have sacrificed all that they hold dear, and this we will not do." [1]

But in view of the eagerness of the West to develop the Soviet ceasefire proposal, Rhee several days later modified his position somewhat. On June 30, 1951, Foreign Minister Y. T. Pyun announced that the Republic of Korea was prepared to participate in any ceasefire, providing the following "clear-cut conditions" were satisfied:

[1] *Pacific Stars & Stripes,* June 25, 1951.

1. Withdrawal of the Chinese Communist armies from Korea.

2. Disarmament of the North Korean Communists.

3. U.N. assurances to prevent "any third power" from giving aid to the North Koreans.

4. The Republic of Korea to participate fully in any international conference dealing with Korean problems.

5. No plan which conflicted with the territorial integrity of Korea (unification) would have legal effect.[2]

These conditions were unrealistic, in view of the fact the armed, unbeaten Chinese Communist foe still bestraddled his country. But to Rhee, the only reality in life was that of a united, independent Korea—the goal he had sought for more than forty years. However, before the invasion of June 1950, he could only vaguely hope for eventual "redemption of our conquered northland." His dream seemed ended forever when the North Korean armies crashed the 38th parallel and sent him fleeing south. United States intervention brought enormous hope until the portentous Chinese Communist intervention. The events of the winter of 1950–51, following Peiping's entrance into the war, once more demonstrated to the embittered Koreans that their lives and destiny lay in the hands of others. "Washington, Moscow and Peiping held the key to Korea's future," wrote Louise Yim. "We were only living puppets; try as we might, move as we would, tug and tear as we could, the strings ran to Washington, Moscow and Peiping." [3]

It is little wonder that a despairing Rhee denounced the proposed peace talks when they began and continued his opposition throughout 1952 and into 1953. Rhee said:

[2] Y. T. Pyun, *Korea—My Country* (Washington: Korean Pacific Press, 1953), p. 148.

[3] Yim, *op. cit.*, p. 294.

"We want all our friends and our enemies alike to know that we must be permitted to utilize every possible means to survive as an independent, unified, democratic nation— even if we have to carry on the struggle alone." [4] A truce, he warned, would mean defeat, a "national death sentence" for Korea. "Without unification," he declared, "economic viability would be next to impossible for Korea." [5]

Rhee's position was clear but the government of the United States was committed to a ceasefire. Initially, in view of the long, arduous task of trying to reach agreement with the Communists, and in the days when it seemed agreement would never be attained, Rhee's stand was of little importance. However when in April 1953 the negotiations at Panmunjom began once again and an armistice appeared imminent, the problem of South Korean non-concurrence loomed up in the path of the negotiations.

General Clark's relationship with Rhee had been excellent "right up to the moment the United States indicated clearly it intended to go through with the armistice that might leave his country divided and the northern portion in the hands of Chinese Communist troops." [6] From that moment on, Clark bore the brunt of Rhee's anger and chagrin. The U.N. commander, together with Ambassador to Korea Ellis O. Briggs,* commenced an exploration of every avenue of argument in an effort to win over the old man to a ceasefire.

The Rhee crisis began on April 24—two days before the resumption of the truce talks—when the Korean informed Eisenhower that he would withdraw his Korean

---

[4] *Korea's Fight for Freedom, Selected Addresses by Korean Statesmen,* Vol. II (Washington: The Korean Pacific Press, 1952), p. 6.

[5] *U.S. News & World Report,* March 7, 1952, interview with Syngman Rhee, pp. 54-58.

[6] Clark, *op. cit.,* p. 257.

* He succeeded Muccio in the fall of 1952.

forces from the United Nations command if any armistice was signed permitting the Chinese Communists to remain south of the Yalu river. Rhee had placed these forces under General MacArthur's command on July 15, 1950. It was obvious that such a withdrawal, and perhaps a South Korean attempt to march alone, would prove disastrous to the entire effort in Korea. Rhee's threat sent Clark flying promptly to Seoul for a lengthy and acrimonious conference, in which the general sought to convince the ROK president of the futility of demanding the unilateral withdrawal of the Chinese. Rhee was unmoved by Clark's arguments.

In the days and weeks that followed Rhee aroused the Korean populace to march in noisy demonstrations protesting the signing of an armistice. On May 12, Clark called upon Rhee to explain the United States position once more, but found him "angrier and more anti-Armistice than ever." The ROK president further informed Clark that he would not allow Communist members of the proposed repatriation commission to operate in South Korea in any armistice, nor would he allow on South Korean soil the Indian troops, who were to take charge of war prisoners for 120 days.

While Rhee balked, Clark was still continuing his pursuit of the elusive armistice agreement at Panmunjom—where the Communists were becoming more and more difficult. On May 13 the American delegation offered several new proposals to the Communists. One of these called for the release of all *Korean* nonrepatriate prisoners on the day of the armistice, with freedom to settle wherever they desired either in North or South Korea. Nam Il "blew up" on hearing this proposal. He declared it to be "a step backwards" in the negotiations. The two delegations argued over the proposal for days, but failed to resolve the matter. On May 16 the U.N. Command recessed the conference once again.

Rhee greeted this evidence of disagreement with satisfaction; but the Americans were at the end of their patience. Clark felt the time had come to test whether the Communists really wanted an armistice or not. He therefore proposed to Washington that he be authorized to place before the Communists the final United States position, to accept or reject it. Washington felt the same way and there now began an important exchange of messages between the Pentagon and Clark's headquarters in Tokyo to determine what this final stand would be. Concurrently, the State Department contacted the various U.N. allies and explained the plan to make a final offer.

On May 23 the Pentagon forwarded to Clark his government's final position. Clark was instructed, against his wishes, to agree to the Communist plan to turn over to the repatriation commission all Korean as well as Chinese nonrepatriate prisoners for the explanation period. Other detailed instructions on the final negotiations were given. But, most important of all, the Washington directive stated that if the Communists rejected this final offer and made no constructive proposal of their own, Clark was authorized to break off all negotiations and undertake to wage an all-out war.

As for the South Korean obstacle, Clark was further directed to confer with Rhee the same day the final offer was being presented to the Communists. He was to explain the offer and also deliver a personal message from President Eisenhower which outlined details of an American plan for economic and military aid to South Korea—if Rhee agreed to the ceasefire.

An hour before the armistice delegations gathered at

Panmunjom on May 25, Clark and Ambassador Briggs met in Seoul with Rhee and Foreign Minister Pyun. The Americans explained the situations, promising in return for South Korea's cooperation the following:

1. An announcement would be made by the sixteen nations which fought in Korea guaranteeing they would band together should the Communists violate the truce in Korea, and that the renewed hostilities might not be confined to Korea.

2. The United States would build up the Republic of Korea army to twenty combat divisions, with appropriate air and naval strength.

3. The United States would initiate an economic aid program to rehabilitate the peninsula, a billion dollar project (but subject to congressional approval).

4. American troops would be kept on the alert in and near Korea until peace was established.[7]

Rhee listened to the Americans with great emotion and then, in a "storm of oratory," he assailed the United States plan. Again he insisted on the withdrawal of the Chinese. "There can be no peaceful settlement without that," he said. "Your threats have no effect upon me. We want to live. We want to survive. We will decide our own fate. Sorry, I cannot assure President Eisenhower of my co-operation under the circumstances."[8] Clark and Briggs argued fruitlessly for several hours, but Rhee and Pyun were unconvinced.

It is doubtful that relations between the two countries had ever been worse. In the days that followed, Rhee ordered Major General Choi Duk Shim, the South Korean delegate at the armistice conference, to boycott the renewed

[7] *Ibid.*, p. 269.
[8] *Ibid.*, p. 270.

discussions. He also released details of the latest American offer to the Communists and the Korean press promptly denounced the offer as "dishonorable and surrendering." [9] Koreans and Americans looked at each other, estranged.

Rhee now decided to make another personal appeal to Eisenhower. On May 30 he wrote the President, declaiming again against an armistice which would leave the Chinese Communists in Korea. He offered a new plan, that there be a simultaneous withdrawal of all foreign troops from Korea "on the condition that a mutual defense pact between our two governments precede it." This pact, he said, should contain the following points:

The United States will agree to come to our military aid and assistance immediately without any consultation or conference with any nation or nations, if and when an enemy nation or nations resume aggressive activities against the Korean peninsula.

The Security Pact should include the United States help in the increase of the ROK armed forces. If we come to agree with the Soviets to refrain from building up the defense forces on both sides, our hands will be tied while the Soviets continue to do it anyway.

Adequate supplies of arms, ammunition, and general logistic materials will be given Korea with a view to making it strong enough to defend itself without needing American soldiers to fight in Korea again.

The United States air and naval forces will remain where they are now so as to deter the enemy from attempting another aggression. [10]

The revolutionary idea of an American defense pact with Korea had been discussed already within the United States. Indeed, President Eisenhower made the decision to offer

[9] *Nippon Times,* May 28, 1953.
[10] U.S. Congress, Senate, *The United States and the Korean Problem,* pp. 81-83.

the pact to the Republic of Korea. Clark and Briggs were informed of this, but they agreed not to broach the subject with Rhee, pending receipt of the Communist answer to the United States final truce offer.

On June 4, 1953, the Communists gave their answer, agreeing on all major points. It seemed that a ceasefire finally was at hand.

On June 6 Eisenhower replied to Rhee's letter. He informed the Korean leader that, after the conclusion and acceptance of an armistice by South Korea, he was ready to negotiate a mutual defense treaty with Rhee. Eisenhower again promised that the United States would continue economic aid and would stand by Korea; he urged Rhee to accept the impending armistice. The most significant statement in Eisenhower's letter was that:

The unification of Korea is an end to which the United States is committed, not once but many times, through its World War II declarations and through its acceptance of the principles enunciated in reference to Korea by the United Nations. Korea is unhappily not the only country that remains divided after World War II. We remain determined to play our part in achieving the political union of all countries so divided. But we do not intend to employ war as an instrument to accomplish the worldwide political settlements to which we are dedicated and which we believe to be just. . . .[11]

General Clark, on visiting Rhee after the Communists' answer of June 4 became known, found the ROK chief executive alternating "between despair and defiance." Rhee informed Clark that thereafter he would feel free to take any action he deemed appropriate. To Clark this meant two possible Korean moves: (1) release of the nonrepatriate POWs, who were guarded for the most part by Korean personnel; and (2) withdrawal of the ROK army from his

11 *Ibid.*, pp. 83-85.

command. Clark managed to elicit a vague promise from Rhee to notify the U.N. Command in advance of any move made by the South Korean government.[12]

On June 9 a report was heard in Seoul that the South Koreans planned to take action to release the nonrepatriate war prisoners.[13] Eisenhower, in hopes of forestalling any drastic action, invited Rhee to Washington to discuss mutual problems. Rhee turned the invitation down, pleading he was too busy. Busy he was, planning the release of the war prisoners. During the early morning hours of June 18, the South Korean guards at prisoner enclosures opened the gates, cut wires, fired weapons into the air, ignited fires, and in devious ways aided some 25,000 nonrepatriate prisoners to stream out into the Korean night.[14] In succeeding days additional hundreds of prisoners also escaped. Rhee had set the stage for an abrupt end to the armistice negotiations.

The Communists, when they heard of the prisoner release, reacted as Rhee had hoped: they promptly broke off the negotiations at Panmunjom, charging the Americans with complicity in the prisoner release.

A devastating wave of world criticism descended upon Rhee and the South Korean government. From almost every capital Rhee was attacked and denounced. Winston Churchill publicly scored Rhee's "treachery" and said flatly that the United Nations had no intention of going forward to conquer all of Korea for him. General Clark, whose troops were dashing around trying to recover some of the prisoners, dispatched a letter to Rhee denouncing "this unilateral abrogation of your personal commitment" not to take any action without first informing him. Clark also

[12] Clark, *op. cit.*, pp. 275-276.
[13] *Nippon Times,* June 10, 1953.
[14] *Ibid.*, June 19, 1953.

ordered General Harrison to dispatch a factual report to the Communist high command, placing the full blame for the release on the Republic of Korea.

While the uproar continued, on June 19 Communist liaison officers passed a letter to the U.N. delegation at Panmunjom, addressed to General Clark. In this letter they bluntly asked: "Is the United Nations Command able to control the Syngman Rhee clique? If not, does the armistice in Korea include the Syngman Rhee clique? If it is not included, what assurance is there for the implementation of the Armistice Agreement on the part South Korea?" [15]

To find the answer, on June 22, Clark flew once more to Seoul. On this occasion, he found the Korean president very nervous and under considerable strain. The general again urged Rhee to reconcile himself to the situation and accept the truce. Rhee, sensitive to the world criticism, remarked that while his government could not sign an armistice which divided his country, it could support such an armistice. This statement, Clark felt, was of utmost importance.[16]

Meanwhile, from Washington, reinforcements in the Rhee negotiations—in the form of Assistant Secretary of State Walter Robertson—arrived in Tokyo. The Robertson mission had been planned before the prisoner release incident. Now, Robertson, Clark, Ambassadors Briggs and Robert Murphy (U.S. Ambassador to Japan) held a top-level conference in Tokyo to decide a future course of action. They decided to recommend to Washington that they proceed "full steam ahead" to sign the armistice. They further recommended that Clark be authorized to reply as

[15] Letter from Communist High Command to General Clark, June 19, 1953, in *Soviet News*, June 25, 1953 (Published by the Press department, Soviet Embassy, London), p. 7.

[16] Clark, *op. cit.*, p. 284.

quickly as possible to the questions posed by the Communists (i.e., did the armistice include Rhee). Washington approved. On June 29 General Clark addressed Kim Il Sung and Peng Teh-huai as follows (excerpts):

The United Nations Command agrees, of course, that the escape of about 25,000 captured personnel of the Korean People's Army is a serious incident and unfortunately has not been conducive to the early armistice for which both sides have been earnestly striving. The United Nations Command, by means of General Harrison's letter of 18 June 1953, immediately informed you of the facts regarding the loss of these prisoners. . . .

In replying to the questions which you asked in your letter, I believe that you realize the armistice which both of us seek is a military armistice between the military commanders of both sides. The United Nations Command is a military command and, contrary to the opinion indicated in your letter of 19 June, does not exercise authority over the Republic of Korea, which is an independent sovereign state. . . . In this incident, that Government violated its commitment, issuing orders which were unknown to me, through other than recognized military channels to certain Korean army units, which permitted the prisoners to escape.

You also asked whether the armistice in Korea included the Republic of Korea as represented by President Syngman Rhee; another question, which is closely related, expressed your interest in knowing what assurances there may be for the implementation of the armistice agreement on the part of South Korea. It is necessary here to reiterate that the armistice which we seek is a military armistice between the commanders of both sides and involving the forces available to the commanders of both sides.

It is recognized that certain provisions of the armistice agreement require the cooperation of the authorities of the Republic of Korea. Where necessary the United Nations Command will, to the limits of its ability, establish military safe-guards to insure that the armistice terms are observed. . . .[17]

While Clark's letter, which recommended the delegations meet at once and proceed with the armistice signing, was being dispatched, Robertson flew off to Seoul to begin a sixteen-day effort to win the formal concurrence of Rhee. Beginning June 25 Robertson began a daily round of discussions with Rhee and ROK advisors, seeking some sort of written pledge that South Korea would abide by the terms of an armistice. Rhee, in the beginning, was apparently unchanged, repeating his old arguments that a divided Korea would be Korea's ultimate death.

The Communists remained plainly incredulous over the spectacle in Seoul. Said *Soviet News*:

But who can earnestly believe, even for a moment, that real power in South Korea is in the grasp of this handful of puppets and not in the hands of the American military command. . . . Who can believe that the miserable hireling Syngman Rhee would take it upon himself to remove 29,000 prisoners of war from the camps . . . if the American military authorities who controlled these prisoners opposed this action? . . .

Nothing was heard of Syngman Rhee for three years. For three years all the affairs in South Korea were directed solely by the American Commander-in-Chief while Syngman Rhee was lodged somewhere in the backyards of the American rear at Pusan. . . . Then suddenly, to the astonishment of the whole world, Syngman Rhee is proclaimed to be so strong and powerful that neither the "U.N. Command," nor the President of the U.S.A. and the U.S. Congress can cope with him. An indecent farce is being enacted. . . .[18]

The U.N. Command could wish it were so, as it explored a number of avenues by which they could bring pressure

[17] U.S. Congress, Senate, *The United States and the Korean Problem*, pp. 93-95.
[18] *Soviet News*, July 16, 1953.

upon Rhee, one of which was a public announcement by Clark that he was preparing to go ahead and sign the armistice without the Koreans.

On July 8 the Communists replied to Clark's letter. Although "not entirely satisfied" with the U.N. commander's letter, they agreed to proceed with the armistice signing. At the same time the Chinese Communist forces began what was to be their last offensive of war, a frontal assault on two Republic of Korean divisions which later spread across the front to include three other ROK divisions. In this last offensive of the war, the South Koreans suffered heavy casualties. Clark sent American divisions into action and the offensive was ended. Clark later stated his belief that one of the main goals of the Chinese offensive was to demonstrate to the South Koreans that a march to the north would be a difficult affair.

Too many forces were against Rhee. The powerful Chinese offensive, the worldwide criticism, the steady American pressure—all worked upon the Korean president. At last, reluctantly, he gave in. On July 11 he told Robertson he would go along with the ceasefire. In return, Robertson promised Rhee the following:

1. A United States-Republic of Korea mutual security pact to be negotiated.

2. Long-term American economic aid.

3. United States agreement to withdraw from the post-armistice political conference after ninety days, should no concrete achievement be made toward peaceful unification in Korea.

4. Expansion of the Republic of Korea army.

By July 20 the Chinese offensive had sputtered out and the way was cleared for speedy implementation of an armistice. On July 27, 1953, at 10 A.M., Generals Harrison and Nam Il signed the armistice agreement. General Clark, and Kim Il Sung and Peng Teh-huai signed at their respective rear headquarters. Twelve hours later the guns fell silent in the Korean hills. The shooting war had ended.

# 14

## The Uneasy Armistice

THE WAR had ended—but not the struggle for Korea. During the first year of the post-armistice period, both sides maneuvered in hopes of gaining what three years of war had not gained them. The political conference, which was to follow the military truce, was held belatedly at Geneva, Switzerland, and proved abortive. Korea thus remained unnaturally divided as ever—this time along a strip of land known as the demilitarized zone (DZ) which, set mostly above the old 38th parallel border, ran a zig-zag course from sea to sea. On both sides of this zone, the armies postured and dug in.

The armistice created a number of immediate problems that had to be speedily resolved. Foremost was the disposition of the prisoners of war over whom so much blood and treasure had been shed. During the first few weeks after the ceasefire, the U.N. Command began the mass movement of more than 70,000 North Korean and Chinese Communist prisoners from their southern camps to the DZ for repatriation. This operation, known as "Big Switch," moved fairly swiftly, marred only by unruly behavior by some of the fanatical Communist prisoners as they went north. By September 1953, all these prisoners had returned to Communist control. For their part, the Communists repatriated 3597 Americans, 7848 South Koreans, 1312 prisoners of other nationalities, and three "Japanese" houseboys. Included among the Americans was a haggard General Dean.

The small number of its returnees worried the U.N. Command. Information obtained from numerous sources, including the prisoners repatriated in "Little Switch" in April, indicated that the Communists held back some prisoners, including American jet pilots. The U.N. protested to the Communists, who blandly insisted they had repatriated all prisoners. Subsequent events showed the Communists had lied, retaining a number of Americans for political purposes.

"Big Switch" was followed by movement into retention camps in the DZ of 22,600 nonrepatriate North Korean and Chinese prisoners from the south, and 359 U.N. prisoners, including 23 Americans, from the north. The Americans were forced to airlift 5000 troops of the Indian Custodial Force by helicopter from Inchon to the camps, as a result of Rhee's opposition to the Indian government which he termed "pro-Communist." By September 24, the Indians and the prisoners were in place.

There now began, in accordance with the armistice agreement, 120 days of "explanations," held under the supervision of the Repatriation Commission headed by Indian Lieutenant General K. S. Thimayya. Much prestige was involved: the United States had insisted the prisoners voluntarily refused to return; the Communists, that they had been forcibly retained. Fortunately for the U.N. Command, the bulk of the prisoners remained loyal to their original choice. The Communists' explanations, at those times when they could get the prisoners to listen to them, were unsuccessful, and only a few prisoners chose to return to them. However, U.N. efforts to win back its people also failed, although two Americans and seven Koreans (out of 359) claimed the right to return during the period.

In early January 1954, as the 120-day deadline for release of the prisoners approached, nerves grew taut in Korea once again. The world also watched worriedly, since the Communists insisted that the prisoners be held for disposition by the political conference on Korea because, they said, the explanations had not been concluded. Said Chou En-lai:

We deem that what is called for today is definitely not to terminate the explanations and release the prisoners of war, but to convene speedily the Political Conference on Korea to seek out a settlement of the question of the disposition of the prisoners of war; moreover, no matter when the Political Conference will be convened, explanations by both sides should be made up for.[1]

However, the U.N. Command had promised the prisoners they would be held no longer than 120 days. General John E. Hull, who succeeded General Clark in October, 1953, declared that he would, as U.N. commander, release the nonrepatriates "at the zero hour of January 23, at which time they would be regarded as displaced persons and helped to go wherever they chose." [2]

The Indians, caught between the Communist and U.N. crossfires, decided they could not make a decision. They therefore declared that their legal responsibilities for the prisoners would end after 120 days (on January 23) and that they would return them to the original detaining sides. This was done and the U.N. command, at one minute after midnight January 23, 1954, promptly declared the prisoners to be "civilians." The nonrepatriates marched out of their compounds and were turned over to the Chinese Nationalist government, in the case of Chinese prisoners, and to the Republic of Korea, in the case of the

[1] *Soviet News,* January 15, 1954.
[2] *Nippon Times,* January 13, 1954.

Koreans. In this way, after their tortuous adventures, some 22,000 prisoners won their freedom.

The victory had gone to the United States. The Communists protested loudly, as usual, and threatened to refuse to accept from the Indians the U.N. prisoners who also had refused repatriation. However, they later relented and these U.N. prisoners, including twenty-one young Americans, disappeared into North Korea.[3] On February 22, its mission ended, the Neutral Nations Repatriation Commission was liquidated. President Eisenhower dispatched a letter to Prime Minister Jawaharlal Nehru, thanking him for the successful handling of the delicate operation by the Indian force. Rhee also was pleased by the outcome and he relented in his opposition to the Indians long enough to permit them to travel by land through South Korea enroute to their homeland.

As we noted earlier, among the promises the United States made to Rhee for agreeing not to oppose an armistice were: (1) economic aid; (2) a sixteen-power declaration of intention to come to South Korea's aid in the event of a new aggression; (3) a mutual defense pact; and (4) withdrawal from the political conference after ninety days.

On the first two promises, the United States acted quickly. The day the truce was signed, President Eisenhower requested Congress to begin immediately a program of expanded aid to South Korea for rehabilitation and economic support. While the long-range program was being worked out, the President asked for an interim authorization of $200 million.[4] Grateful that the war had ended, Congress speedily passed the bill.

[3] A number of these Americans later voluntarily returned to the United States.
[4] Press release, July 27, 1953, President's Message to Congress.

In addition, on July 27, the sixteen nations that had fought in Korea signed a "Joint Policy Declaration Concerning the Korean Armistice," in which they affirmed that if there were a renewal of the armed attack, they would be prompt again in resisting aggression and that: "The consequence of such a breach of the armistice would be so grave that, in all probability, it would not be possible to confine hostilities within the frontiers of Korea." [5]

The American government also moved to make good its promise to Rhee concerning the important mutual defense pact—which was to place the United States on the Asian mainland. Promptly after the signing of the truce, Secretary of State Dulles flew to Seoul to negotiate the actual treaty. In the document which resulted, the most important sentence, Article III, stated:

Each Party recognizes that an armed attack in the Pacific Area on either of the Parties in territories now under their respective administrative control, or hereafter recognized by one of the Parties as lawfully brought under the administrative control of the other, would be dangerous to its own peace and safety and declares that it would act to meet the common danger in accordance with its constitutional processes. [6]

On August 7, 1953, Rhee and Dulles initialed a draft of the treaty. In a joint statement issued after the ceremony, the two pledged continued cooperation between their countries and agreed that in the political conference which was to follow (according to the armistice, within three months), they would "seek to achieve the peaceful unification of historic Korea as a free and independent nation." They added that if it appeared, after ninety days, that attempts to

[5] State Department, *Joint Policy Declaration Concerning the Korean Armistice,* Signed at Washington, July 27, 1953 (Washington: Government Printing Office, 1953), p. 2.

[6] Press release, Draft of Republic of Korea-United States Mutual Defense Treaty, August 7, 1953.

achieve mutual objectives were fruitless, both countries would make "a concurrent withdrawal from the conference" and then would "consult further regarding the attainment of a unified, free and independent Korea. . . ." [7]

A final draft of the treaty was initialed in Washington on October 1 by Dulles and Foreign Minister Pyun. In January 1954, Dulles presented the proposal to the Senate foreign relations committee. In his remarks to the committee, Dulles said the treaty was a logical outgrowth of the successful joint efforts to repel the Communist invasion. Its primary value "consists in giving the Communists notice, beyond any possibility of misinterpretation, that the United States would not be indifferent to any new Communist aggression in Korea. It is our hope that this reaffirmation will, in combination with other measures which we are taking in the Far East, disabuse the Communists of any ideas of launching another aggression in Korea." [8]

After several weeks the Senate voted eighty-one to six for approval of the Treaty—but it stipulated that the United States would not support any aggressive South Korean military moves to unify Korea by force.

Meanwhile at Panmunjom, the Communist and U.N. armistice delegations had continued to meet to make arrangements for the political conference. To represent the U.N. in the negotiations, the United States dispatched Ambassador Arthur H. Dean. The Communists, in their meetings with Dean, reverted to their former delaying tactics, insisting once more that the Soviet Union must be included in the conference as a neutral participant. On December 13, Dean walked out of the conference after an

[7] Press release, Joint Statement of President Rhee and Secretary Dulles, August 7, 1953.

[8] Press release, Dulles Statement before Senate Foreign Relations Committee, January 13, 1954.

abusive session in which the Communists charged the United States with "perfidy" in the armistice arrangements. The negotiations went into a state of suspension, although a State Department official remained behind at Panmunjom.

It was not until February 1954 that further progress was made toward the convening of the political conference. This came about following meetings in Berlin of the foreign ministers of the Big Three. On February 18 they agreed to call a conference at Geneva on April 26 to discuss the Korean problem. They additionally scheduled for discussion "the problem of restoring peace in Indochina." [9]

The Geneva meeting in April soon made clear the impossibility of reconciling the divergent views on how to unite Korea—or who was to do it. But even as the Korean problem was being discussed, the attention of the world shifted to Southeast Asia and the rising crescendo of fighting in Indochina. There the French found themselves besieged in the northern Indochina fortress of Dien Bien Phu by their former Communist guerrilla foe, now a well-armed, modernized Viet Minh army. The French appealed to the United States for aid and the American government responded with vast quantities of supplies and equipment, and even tottered momentarily on the brink of direct United States military intervention. Finally, on May 7, 1954, the decimated Dien Bien Phu fortress fell, and with it a French cabinet and northern Indochina. The Communists had won an important victory.

In Korea, Syngman Rhee stirred restlessly. As the Indochina crisis reached its peak, he pointed an accusing finger at his American allies, complaining that the Indochina de-

[9] State Department, *The Korean Problem at the Geneva Conference,* April 26-June 15, 1954 (Washington: Government Printing Office, 1954), p. 5.

feat might never have happened if a Korean victory had been achieved, since it was clear Peiping had greatly increased logistical support to the Viet Minh. Indeed, the Americans themselves began to doubt the wisdom of the decision not to seek military victory in Korea; the shades of MacArthur's "no substitute for victory" strategy arose to trouble them. Rhee, convinced more than ever that his policies were right, offered to send two ROK army divisions to aid the French in Indochina. The offer was rejected by the U.N. command.

At Geneva the Korean phase of the conference ended in a deadlock. The sixteen U.N. nations summed up negotiations in a declaration on June 15, 1954, in which they pointed out that the Communists had rejected

our every effort to obtain agreement. The principal issues between us therefore are clear. Firstly, we accept and assert the authority of the United Nations. The Communists repudiate and reject the authority and competence of the United Nations in Korea and have labelled the United Nations itself as the tool of aggression. Were we to accept this position of the Communists, it would mean the death of the principle of collective security and of the United Nations itself. Secondly, we desire genuinely free elections. The Communists insist upon procedures which would make genuinely free elections impossible. It is clear that the Communists will not accept impartial and effective supervision of free elections. Plainly, they have shown their intention to maintain Communist control over North Korea. They have persisted in the same attitudes which have frustrated United Nations efforts to unify Korea since 1947.

We believe, therefore, that it is better to face the fact of our disagreement than to raise false hopes and mislead the peoples of the world into believing that there is agreement where there is none.[10]

[10] *Ibid.*, pp. 191-192.

The political conference had failed, just as Rhee had predicted, and the ROK president said "I told you so" to his American allies. Once more, he reiterated that only force would unite Korea.

A solution to the Korean problem seemed unattainable. President Eisenhower, in accordance with previous American promises to consult with the Koreans should the political conference fail, now invited Rhee to visit Washington. Rhee accepted, and late in July 1954, the 79-year-old patriot flew to Washington with an entourage of military and political advisers. Rhee had made plans to appeal his case directly to the American people. On July 28, 1954—a year after the ceasefire—he appeared before a joint session of the United States Congress and called for all-out war against the Communists.

"There is little time," he warned. "Within a few years the Soviet Union will possess the means to vanquish the United States. We must act now." Communist China, he assured the Congress, was "a monster with feet of clay," vulnerable to blockade. As for Soviet Russia, Rhee said it "would not dare to risk war with the United States" if victory was won in Korea and Indochina. But even if the Soviet government did decide to go to war, the Korean leader said, that would be "excellent for the free world, since it would justify the destruction of the Soviet centers of production by the American Air Force before the Soviet hydrogen bombs had been produced in quantity. . . ." [11]

Rhee's call for a preventive war met no favorable echo from the Congress or the American people.

[11] *The New York Times,* July 28, 1954.

# 15

# Rebellion Again and a Fall from Power

IN AUGUST 1954, after trips to New York, Philadelphia and other American cities across the country, the fiery Korean leader returned to his battered homeland. During his conversations with the Americans, ignoring the negative reaction to his congressional address, Rhee had continued to call for a renewed war to push back the Communists. "Korea cannot survive as either north or south alone," he argued, "each must have the other. We cannot wait for the unnatural death division means . . . We have cooperated with the United States, but that has now come to an end. . . ." [1]

Rhee's warning that he might again oppose U.S. policy was dismissed in Washington, where the administration was preparing plans to withdraw a substantial portion of U.S. forces from the peninsula. These plans were disclosed to Rhee's entourage during the Washington meetings; however, the withdrawal clearly had been foreshadowed as early as December 1953 when President Eisenhower announced that two of the eight American divisions in Korea would be recalled.* The redeployment of these forces was an integral part of the Eisenhower "New Look" defense policy, which was to emphasize nuclear air power over other forces to deter future aggression.

[1] *The New York Times,* August 1, 1954.

* These units, the 40th and 45th divisions, departed Korea in the spring of 1954.

Rhee not only was distressed by the troop withdrawal plan, which would shut the door on his hopes of unifying Korea by force, but also by a related American policy aimed at strengthening Japan as the nucleus of a new alliance between Tokyo, Seoul and Taipei. The old patriarch, who had struggled so many years against the Japanese, could not forget the bitter days of his youth, nor the events of 1905 when, in his words, President Theodore Roosevelt "betrayed Korea" and agreed to Japan's seizure of the country. The Japanese, he continued to insist, could not be trusted.

Beset by these anxieties and fears, Rhee returned to South Korea on August 13, 1954 determined to oppose the Americans once again. Two days later, in an address to a gathering of Koreans in front of the capitol building on the ninth anniversary of the country's liberation from Japan, Rhee sounded his old war cry. The Republic of Korea, he said, had prepared a new military plan which would unite the country "without great sacrifice" and without the use "of atomic or hydrogen bombs." He stated that when the time was ripe, the ROK army would march northward "in a great crusade and campaign" that would lead "to victory and peace." [2]

In Washington Rhee's words evoked concern that he might yet manage to destroy the armistice. However, in some American circles—notably among retired high-ranking U.S. military leaders who had participated in the Korean campaign—Rhee could find encouragement for his stand against Washington. On August 10, for example, the former U.N. commander in the Far East, General Mark Clark, told a congressional investigating committee that: "Mr. Rhee thought that the only solution was to

[2] *Nippon Times,* August 16, 1954.

unify (Korea) by military means and I guess he is right."
General Clark argued that the United States should have
pursued victory, that: "We should fight to win, and we
should not go in for a limited war." [3] These were the same
sentiments Rhee had expressed on numerous occasions.

Other retired military officers testified in a similar vein.
The former Air Force commander in Tokyo, Lt. Gen.
George E. Stratemeyer, complained that the American
forces in Korea simply had "not been permitted to win." [4]
General James Van Fleet, appearing before the committee
several weeks later, said: ". . . everybody in the Eighth
army, to include our United Nations allies and the
Koreans, believed in victory and believed they could
achieve victory. I still believe we could have achieved
victory in Korea." [5] One famous voice was publicly silent,
but at his residence in New York's Waldorf Towers, General MacArthur during conversations with friends denounced America's Korean policies, past and present.

Worried by the continuing criticisms from these officers,
and the possibility Rhee might try to rekindle the war,
on August 18 Washington announced somewhat hur-
riedly that four of the six remaining divisions in Korea
would be recalled. Nine days later the U.S. Air Force also
reported plans to redeploy aircraft units from Korea to
Japan, and the British and Canadian governments said
they would reduce their military contributions to the U.N.
Command. The implication of these announcements was
clear: if Rhee was determined to march to the north, he
would have to march alone.

[3] U.S. Congress, Senate, *Interlocking Subversion in Government Departments,* Hearings Before the Subcommittee . . . of the Committee of the
Judiciary, 82d Cong., 2d Sess. (Washington: Government Printing Office,
1954), Part 21, pp. 1703-1704.

[4] *Ibid.,* Part 22, p. 1724.

[5] *Ibid.,* Part 24, p. 2028.

Although the previous withdrawal of the two American divisions should have softened the blow for the South Korean populace, the news of the impending large-scale U.S. redeployment came as a shock. Taking advantage of the people's fears, the Korean government now attacked the United States for "abandoning" Korea. The National Assembly went into emergency session and, adopting a resolution denouncing the withdrawal, warned Washington that its plan would encourage a new Communist assault. In Seoul giant public rallies were organized by the Rhee government, and the people paraded in front of the U.S. embassy and Eighth army headquarters compounds, demanding that the troops remain in the country.

American embassy and military officials tried, without much success, to reassure the people. General Maxwell D. Taylor (Van Fleet's successor as Eighth army commander) pointed out that a planned build-up of the ROK army to 20 divisions, together with the remaining U.S. and U.N. forces, would provide the same number of frontline divisions that existed on armistice day.[6] General Hull, the United Nations commander, reminded the Koreans that the U.S. and its allies were firmly pledged to come immediately to South Korea's assistance in the event of a new aggression. "The United Nations Command," General Hull said, "still has the same responsibility for the security of Korea. We have not abandoned Korea."[7]

During the height of the anti-troop withdrawal agitation, negotiations between Washington and Seoul over future American military and economic aid programs—which had been underway for many weeks—reached a

[6] *Tokyo Mainichi*, September 5, 1954.
[7] *Nippon Times*, September 17, 1954.

complete deadlock. One of the major issues in these negotiations was Rhee's demand that the U.S. help South
Korea double the size of the ROK army to 40 divisions,
which was rejected. Other U.S.-Korean issues involved:
(a) Rhee's refusal to establish a more realistic rate of
exchange between the local currency (hwan) and the
U.S. dollar; and (b) his rejection of an American demand
that aid funds be partly used to purchase goods in Japan.

On October 1, 1954, continuing his defiance of the
United States, the Korean leader halted all hwan advances
to the U.N. Command,* and tightened an economic boycott previously ordered of Japanese trade. Exasperated
by these obstructionist tactics, Washington directed General Hull to use American dollars and post exchange
merchandise to pay his Korean employees, and ordered a
cut-off of all petroleum supplies to South Korea. When
the ROK government protested against these "illegal"
actions, the U.S. issued a warning that unless its proposals
were accepted, future aid to Korea would be imperiled.

As the weeks passed and the impasse between Washington and Seoul continued, Rhee finally realized that his
campaign to change U.S. policies had failed and that, in
fact, it was beginning to undermine South Korea's rehabilitation. He had little choice but to call off his campaign and to make the best of Washington's terms. Thus,
in mid-November, he agreed to the signing of a $700
million American military and economic assistance program to Korea for 1954-1955. It constituted the largest
single U.S. aid program in the world.

Under terms of his agreement, Washington reaffirmed
its pledge to use military force to defend South Korea
against any new Communist attack. It also promised to

* The funds were used to pay the Command's 100,000 Korean employees.

continue the economic aid program in future years, and to help the South Koreans organize a 10-division reserve for the ROK army. On his part, Rhee promised to establish a more realistic hwan-dollar rate of exchange, and to make new efforts to curb inflation and to balance the ROK budget. He also agreed to procure aid supplies from wherever the best price and quality could be obtained— including from his old enemy, Japan.[8]

The 1954 economic and military aid pact did not, however, end all disagreements between the two governments. One of the major issues remaining concerned the status of the neutral nations supervisory commission (NNSC). This agency, created under terms of the armistice, was responsible for monitoring the ceasefire and reporting to each side the results of its "supervision, observation, inspection, and investigation." The NNSC was composed of 20 inspection teams, each being equally divided between nationals from Sweden, Switzerland, Poland and Czechoslovakia.

Almost immediately after the ceasefire, however, it became apparent that the commission was defective. The reason was highlighted by a former Polish military attache, who fled to the West following a North Korean assignment. He wrote:

Whenever an inspection team of Poles, Czechs, Swiss and Swedes went into South Korea to keep an eye on U.N. supply shipments, the Poles and Czechs on the team used the opportunity to collect and photograph all the classified information they could on U.S. tactics, aircrafts, logistics and training.

[8] State Department, *American Foreign Policy, Basic Documents: 1950-1955*, Vol. II (Washington: Government Printing Office, 1957), pp. 2734-2736.

When the teams went to North Korea, the Poles and Czechs did their best to keep the Swedes and Swiss from seeing anything of military value. For example, at Sinuiju and Manpoijin, the two border towns on the Yalu where the Swedes and Swiss wanted to check trains from China for contraband military supplies, the Poles and Czechs worked directly with the very Communist generals they were supposed to be policing. The Chinese and North Koreans informed them whenever a train was coming through loaded with forbidden new weapons. Then the Czechs and Poles would try to lure the Swiss and Swedes away, often by producing a fake train with no freight on it. When the inspectors' backs were turned, the new guns and tanks went rolling south.[9]

The Swiss and Swedes quickly uncovered the deception. In May 1954, in response to U.S. complaints, they reported they had been "constantly and systematically frustrated" by the Communists and thus were unable to perform their duties. Shortly thereafter their two governments recommended to Washington and Peiping that the commission be abolished.

The U.S. endorsed this proposal, but the Communists rejected it. A Swiss writer later noted that: ". . . those who hampered and indeed paralyzed the Neutral Nations Supervisory Commission posed as its most ardent and active defenders, while the representatives of the United Nations Command and the Swedish representatives, who had sought in every way to make the Commission effective, appealed for its abolition." [10] The United States, although tempted to act unilaterally against the Commission, in the

[9] Col. Pawel Monat, "Russians in Korea: The Hidden Bosses," *Life*, Vol. 48 (June 27, 1960), p. 76.

[10] Jacques Freymond, "Supervising Agreements: The Korean Experience," *Foreign Affairs*, Vol. 37, No. 3 (April 1959), pp. 500-501.

end decided to do nothing which might upset the armistice.

To Syngman Rhee the U.S. refusal to act was incomprehensible, in view of the continuing Communist espionage activities. Whereupon, he began a unilateral campaign to harrass the NNSC through mass demonstrations and veiled threats against the physical safety of its members. In August 1954 the National Assembly also was convened to appeal to the United Nations for "an immediate dissolution" of the commission, based on evidence that the Poles and Czechs were spying on South Korea.[11] Later, in November, when these actions brought no results, Rhee issued an ultimatum to the Czechs and Poles to get out of the country within a week's time or face "the most positive measures."

At this juncture, however, the U.N. Command notified the ROK government that General Hull would "use all the means at his disposal" to protect the commission, as required under terms of the armistice.[12] A direct clash was avoided only when Rhee was requested "by the highest United States authorities in Washington," and agreed, to set aside his ultimatum. The request was made by Secretary of State Dulles in connection with a Swedish plan to refer the problem to the Political Committee of the U.N. General Assembly in early December. This action was duly taken, but the Soviet delegate on the committee insisted that the supervisory commission was performing a useful function, and that there was no need at all to reform it.[13] Since under terms of the armistice

---

11 *The New York Times,* August 16, 1954.
12 *Washington Post,* November 23, 1954.
13 Freymond, *op. cit.,* p. 500.

the consent of both sides was required to change any provisions, in the end nothing came of the appeal to the U.N.

The situation continued to gall the South Koreans. "The Communists made a truce at Panmunjon," Rhee complained, "but they started breaking it even before the ink was dry. Nobody denies that these violations are flagrant, violent, and constant. What, then, is the value of a truce if we keep it, but they do not?" [14] To meet Rhee's demands, in the summer of 1955 the United States managed to obtain a limited agreement from the Communists to reduce the number of inspection teams. But Rhee was unimpressed, and on August 5 he issued a new ultimatum to the Communist members of the commission to leave South Korea. To back up his ultimatum, he ordered new mass demonstrations at compounds where the teams were being protected by U.S. troops. These affairs quickly got out of hand, and in the resultant riots more than 50 Americans and 100 Koreans were injured, and one Korean was killed.[15] The incidents led to bitter denunciations by both sides.

In Washington Secretary Dulles, although expressing some sympathy with Rhee's viewpoint, said the United States would continue to oppose all Korean attempts to use force against the commission. The American position was, he said, that the U.N. Command was obligated to protect the NNSC. A week later, however, he revealed that the U.S. and its allies were holding new talks with the Swiss and Swedes on the problem of the commission which, he noted, "may be serving an evil purpose not intended." [16]

14 *Korean Survey,* Vol. 4, No. 7 (October 1955), p. 15.
15 *The New York Times,* August 10, 1955.
16 *Ibid.,* August 17, 1955.

Nine months elapsed before these conversations produced the desired solution. It was achieved after the Swedes proposed that the inspection teams in North and South Korea be temporarily withdrawn, and that reliance be placed on mobile inspection teams operating from the demilitarized zone. This proposal led to a new, and futile, correspondence between the two sides. Finally, on May 31, 1956 the United States announced it would unilaterally suspend all inspections in South Korea until such time as the teams in the north were allowed to carry out their functions.[17]

The Communists objected and denounced the American plan as a violation of the armistice. The U.S. was undeterred and nine days later the inspection teams in South Korea were flown to Panmunjom. On June 10 and 11 the teams in North Korea also were returned to the demilitarized zone, and the objectionable activities of the commission were finally halted.* In Seoul, the 81-year-old Rhee was greatly pleased by this outcome, and by the fact that his American allies had finally acted in the manner which he had been urging for two acrimonious years.

While he was challenging friend and foe alike internationally, the strong-willed Korean leader also was engaged in a serious of domestic quarrels which ultimately led to his downfall. The main issue of these disputes was Rhee's determination to cling to power. Possessed of an almost overweening confidence in his own leadership and ability, Rhee justified his authoritarian rule of the country by

[17] *Ibid.,* June 1, 1956.
* The commission continued to function in the demilitarized zone, but its basic mission was ended.

citing his popularity with the people. This combination of pride and egocentrism, however, coupled with his general intolerance of criticism, created much resentment in opposition circles.

Rhee's first major, but temporary, setback in South Korean politics went back to the spring of 1950, when his Liberal party supporters suffered substantial losses in the Assembly elections. These defeats threatened Rhee's re-election to the presidency, since the Assembly was empowered to choose the nation's chief executive under terms of the ROK constitution.* Fearing a further defeat in 1952, Rhee and his supporters began a campaign to amend the constitution to transfer the election of the president to the people.

This proposal was fought by opposition forces in the Assembly. Finding that he could not gain a two-thirds majority vote for the amendment, Rhee proclaimed a state of martial law and denounced his opponents as "pro-Communists" who had betrayed "the will of the people." This internal crisis, occurring in the midst of the Korean war, was attributed to Rhee's ambition and produced much criticism. Nevertheless, he persisted and on July 5, 1952—through a combination of threats, polemics and coercion—he finally forced the Assembly to adopt the amendment. In the elections that followed a month later he was returned to office by a landslide, winning 7,275,883 votes out of 8,259,428 cast. Although this demonstration of his great popularity with the people lessened American criticism, it did not end the resentment felt by his battered political opponents.

Two years later, in September 1954, Rhee and the

* Rhee had first been elected president by the Assembly on July 19, 1948 by a vote of 180 to 16.

Liberals created a new crisis by demanding the Assembly adopt two more constitutional amendments. One was aimed at removing the two-term restriction on Rhee as the nation's first president, and the other at abolishing the position of premier. In late November, despite a failure to win the necessary two-thirds majority in the Assembly, the Liberals declared the amendments adopted.* Thus in two successive campaigns against his assembly opponents, Rhee had made himself eligible to run for the presidency for life.

The ineffectiveness of his political opposition during these years reflected the anarchical nature of Korean politics. Plagued by dozens of splinter parties and cliques, Rhee's opposition was so constantly engaged in factional disputes it was unable to unite against him. However, in late 1955 his major opponents finally managed to submerge their differences and created a new political organization, the Democratic party. They nominated a former speaker of the Assembly, P. H. Shinicky, as their candidate to run against Rhee in 1956. For vice president, they nominated Dr. John M. Chang, a former ambassador to Washington. Chang's opponent was Lee Ki-Poong, a close friend of Rhee and chairman of the Liberal party.

In drawing up their plans for the 1956 campaign, both major parties realized that because of Rhee's advanced age, the vice presidency might be the key to future political power in South Korea. This expectation, which was an admission that Rhee was unbeatable at the polls, in fact became the Democrat's last hope when their candidate, Shinicky, suddenly died of a heart attack ten days before the election. Left without major opposition, Rhee on May 15 easily won his third term as president. His

* The Liberals claimed victory by one-third of a vote.

margin of victory, however, was substantially below his 1952 total, and indeed in Seoul the dead Shinicky beat him by some 63,000 votes.[18]

In the vice presidential race, on the other hand, John M. Chang pulled an unexpected upset by defeating the Liberal's candidate by some 207,000 votes. This remarkable event—the election of a president and vice president from opposing parties—created "an unprecedented and difficult situation," as Rhee promptly complained. In the days that followed the Liberals sought ways to invalidate Chang's election; however, with U.N. and American observers on the scene, such guile was too much for Rhee. On May 19 he reluctantly announced that he would recognize Chang's accession to the vice presidency.

The elections of 1956 established the power of the Democratic party. However, they also left much enmity in the hearts of the Liberals. Well aware of their feeling, and fearful for his life, Chang went into hiding following his election. The events which followed justified his caution. On August 15, after his inauguration as vice president on the same day Rhee was sworn in, Chang made a speech criticizing the Liberal party administration and three weeks later became the target of an assassin's bullet. Fortunately escaping with only a hand wound, the vice president charged the Liberals with collusion in the assasination attempt,* and went into seclusion once more. For many months thereafter he remained completely isolated from the affairs of the government.

In the years that followed only Rhee's heartbeat barred

[18] *Washington Post*, May 16, 1956.

* Chang's assailant was jailed and eventually put to death. Five years later six officials of the Rhee government, including the minister of home affairs, were convicted for their part in the attempted assassination. They were sentenced to terms ranging from 10 years to life imprisonment.

Chang and the Democrats from taking power. The worried Liberals, concerned over this possibility, tried to amend the constitution again in 1958 to bar Chang from the succession, but were unsuccessful. Rhee's health, however, held up remarkably well, although as the 1960 presidential elections approached, he was nearing his eighty-fifth birthday and it seemed probable he would not survive another four-year term as president.

It was with Rhee's death in mind that the two parties girded themselves for the new elections. To run against him on this occasion, the Democrats nominated Cho Byong Ok, a former national police director, and renominated Chang for vice president. Chang's opponent again became Lee Ki-Poong, the Liberal leader. Early in February 1960, as the campaign got underway, a pernicious fate once again struck down the Democratic presidential candidate. Cho Byong Ok became seriously ill, was flown to the United States for emergency treatment, and died there on February 16. For the second successive time, Rhee was left without major opposition, and, on March 15, won his fourth term as president.

Following Cho's death the attention of the electorate immediately centered on the crucial vice presidential race. However, on this occasion the Liberals had taken precautions to defeat Chang. During the balloting opposition voters were abused by the national police at the polling booths, while in hidden rooms the Liberals were engaged in outright ballot box fraud. When the Democrats complained and organized street protests, the police moved against them and bloody clashes ensued in several South Korean cities. After the ballots were counted, Lee Ki-Poong was proclaimed South Korea's new vice president by more than six million votes.

It was this openly fraudulent vice presidential election that set the stage for Rhee's ouster from power. The angry Democrats promptly filed a suit in the South Korean Supreme Court, demanding nullification of the election, and also sought to organize new demonstrations against the government. Their cause, however, seemed hopeless until they were suddenly presented with an unexpected martyr on April 11. On that day the mutilated body of a young student, missing since election day clashes with Masan city police, was fished from the harbor. For hours afterwards thousands of citizens filed past the body in a hospital. Later, they gathered in the street for a protest march that quickly turned into a riot. Before the Masan demonstrations had run their course, the people had burned a police box, stoned the city hall and police station, and physically assaulted the local police chief and other city officials.

The news of these riots, which continued for several days, was broadcast throughout South Korea and triggered a more violent demonstration in the capital. It began on the morning of April 19, when students from high schools and colleges throughout the city began a march that soon swelled to more than 100,000 people. The police attempted, but failed, to break up the massive demonstration. The unruly mob surged on to the National Assembly building, where it set up a great anti-government clamor.[19]

After several hours some 3,000 demonstrators broke away from the larger group and marched towards the presidential mansion, where police had erected a barbed wire barricade. When the students approached, the police

[19] "The April Revolution," *Korean Report*, Vol. 1, No. 1, (April 1961), p. 5.

opened fire with rifles and tear gas, causing a number of immediate casualties. The sight of their friends falling only aroused the demonstrators more, and they advanced again into the face of repeated volleys of rifle fire. The unequal battle lasted more than an hour, as the students made several attempts to break through to the mansion using two commandeered street cars, a jeep, and a fire truck. When they finally had fled the scene, they left behind more than 110 people dead in the streets, and hundreds of others wounded.

The news of these bloody events in front of Rhee's official residence stunned the Korean people, and caused great concern in the United States. In Seoul the U.S. ambassador, Walter P. McConaughy, issued a statement urging the students to call a halt to their demonstrations, and urging the government to redress the people's "justifiable grievances." In Washington Secretary of State Christian A. Herter took a much stronger position, charging the ROK government with adopting repressive measures "unsuited to a free democracy." [20] Vice president Chang subsequently announced he was resigning from his office four months ahead of schedule in order "to ring bells of warning to the Syngman Rhee government, which is drunk with power." [21]

Within the presidential mansion, Rhee did not seem to immediately grasp the significance of the day's fatal events. Instead, he proclaimed a state of martial law and, charging the riots had been Communist-inspired, ordered ROK army units into the city. During the next few days, how-

[20] State Department, *A Historical Summary of United States-Korean Relations* (Washington: Government Printing Office, 1962), p. 131.

[21] Richard Allen, *Korea's Syngman Rhee: An Unauthorized Portrait* (Rutland, Vt., Charles E. Tuttle, 1960), p. 211.

ever, as a storm of domestic and international criticism swept down upon him, Rhee finally became aware of the seriousness of the crisis.

Seeking to restore calm to a shocked nation, Rhee announced he would meet with several former advisors and elder statesmen to examine the causes of the riots, and consider possible governmental reforms. Two of these men, former Seoul mayor Huh Chung, and former foreign minister Pyun, met with Rhee on April 22 and bluntly informed him that Communist agitation had played no significant part in the rioting. The students, they said, had been protesting the failure of the government to provide for civil liberties.[22]

On April 24 Rhee left the presidential mansion for the first time since the riots and travelled to the National University hospital, where a number of student demonstrators were recovering from their wounds. For an hour, weeping openly, he visited by their bedsides. Afterwards, he issued a statement expressing his deep personal grief. "The terrible tragedy of April 19," he said, "has left a deep scar upon Korea and the hearts of our people. Our beloved nation has been shaken and our prestige in the free world has been grievously damaged. I have no words to express the depths of my sorrow for the shocking loss of life." [23]

Rhee said that he had always believed in strong political parties, but in view of the existing situation, he announced he would "divorce" himself from all such organizations and would "seek to serve the nation solely as its chief executive. . . ." He said that he had accepted the resignation of members of his cabinet, and would ap-

22 *The New York Times,* April 23, 1960.
23 *Ibid.,* April 24, 1960.

point "new and able men" to head up the various departments of the government.

Rhee's statement failed to mollify his opponents, who now saw an opportunity to achieve major governmental changes. On April 25, despite the state of martial law, they organized new street demonstrations—generally orderly—demanding Rhee's resignation and new elections. At nightfall, however, violence flared once again when a group of demonstrators sacked and demolished the car and home of Lee Ki-Poong, the vice president-elect (he and his family took refuge inside the presidential grounds). An ominous note this day for Rhee and his supporters was the friendly attitude and forebearance of the army troops towards the demonstrators.

As the excitement continued, on April 26 Rhee made a major concession, agreeing to call for new elections and announcing that Lee Ki-Poong would be asked to resign from all of his governmental posts. However, public sentiment was running at full tide against the Korean leader. That same day his military adviser, Lt. Gen. Song Yo Chan, persuaded Rhee to meet with a delegation from the streets to hear their demands. Five representatives, including two students, were selected and ushered into his presence. It was an emotional meeting: when they came face to face with the tired, worried old man, they all burst into tears. Nevertheless, they delivered a letter from the demonstrators demanding his resignation, Lee's ouster, and new elections.[24]

During the day the U.S. ambassador also visited Rhee together with General Carter B. Magruder, the United Nations commander, and urged the Korean president to end the crisis by acquiescing in the people's demands.

24 "The April Revolution," *op. cit.*, p. 6.

Almost simultaneously Rhee learned that 136 members of the National Assembly had voted unanimously to request him to resign. Faced by these great pressures, sensing a loss of support in the army, and seeing his own party support evaporate, the "strongman" of South Korea finally agreed to step down. He named Huh Chung to serve as acting premier of a caretaker government pending new elections, and on April 27 issued a one-sentence announcement: "I, Syngman Rhee, honoring the resolution of the National Assembly, resign as president and wish to devote the rest of my life to the nation and people as a citizen." [25]

On news of Rhee's resignation a wild celebration broke out in the city of Seoul. It was still continuing when the "April revolution" reached out the next day to claim four more unexpected victims. Lee Ki-Poong, the chairman of the Liberal party, a man who had seemed destined for a major role in Korean affairs, committed suicide along with his wife and two sons. He acted in apparent atonement for his contribution to Rhee's downfall. That is, except for the rigged vice presidential election, the Korean leader would have gone on to serve his fourth term as president. The tragedy was compounded by the fact that several years earlier Rhee had adopted Lee's elder son.

On April 29, as he drove from the presidential mansion for the last time, Rhee's grief-stricken departure became the occasion for a final personal triumph. Thousands of Koreans who had lined the streets began to applaud as his car passed, and many wept. "He is now a patriot," a young student said. "His resignation proved it. We would not have forgiven him had he not stepped down." [26] Three

[25] Kyung Cho Chung, *New Korea: New Land of the Morning Calm* (New York: Macmillan, 1962), p. 67.
[26] *Los Angeles Times*, April 29, 1960.

weeks later the retired Korean executive flew off to a new exile in Hawaii, and the Rhee era in Korean politics came to an inglorious end.

In Washington, after these events reached their final, peaceful conclusion, President Eisenhower sat down to write a personal letter to Rhee. On a number of prior occasions Eisenhower had privately expressed a wish that the South Koreans would overthrow the stubborn old man and replace him with a more moderate leader.[27] Now the event had occurred, and on May 9, 1960 the President wrote to Rhee to praise him for his "long years of patient and arduous labor" on behalf of his country. "Your tenacity and indomitable courage," he said, "at a time when the Republic was the prey of Communist armies won the admiration of the entire free world as well as the gratitude of all Koreans." Eisenhower assured Rhee that in the future the United States would continue to feel itself bound by strong ties to Korea "under your successors." [28]

[27] Sherman Adams, *First-Hand Report: The Story of the Eisenhower Administration* (New York: Harpers, 1961), p. 101.

[28] *Public Papers of President of the United States, Dwight D. Eisenhower, 1960-1961* (Washington: Government Printing Office, 1961), pp. 401-402.

# 16

## The Rise of the New
## Korean Strongman

WITHIN WEEKS after Rhee's departure, his successors
adopted a new constitution which provided for a bicameral
legislature and transfer of executive power from the president to a prime minister and state council. The office of
president was retained, with provisions made for the in-
cumbent to serve only as titular head of state. On July
29, 1960 new elections for the Assembly were held and
the Democrats emerged with a majority of seats in both
houses. Two weeks later they elected Yun Po Sun, a
founder of the Democratic party, as president for a five
year term. On August 19 John M. Chang was designated as
prime minister.[1] Thus, less than four months after Rhee's
fall from power, the government of the second Republic
of Korea was inaugurated.

Soon after taking over the premiership, Chang turned
his attention to the country's chaotic economic situation,
which he found was worse than he had imagined. Fifteen
years after liberation, the Republic of Korea was bank-
rupt, weighed down by mass poverty, illiteracy and unemployment.* Still suffering from the artificial division of

[1] "Korea's New Government—1960," *Korean Survey*, Vol. 10, No. 1
(January 1961), pp. 3-6.
* With a population estimated at twenty-four million people in 1961,
South Korea was the fifth most densely populated nation in the world—
after the Netherlands, Belgium, Taiwan, and Japan.

the peninsula, South Korea lacked sufficient resources, electric power and water supplies, or major industries.

In an effort to end some of these deficiencies, during the winter of 1960-1961 the Chang government drew up a plan for a long-range $30 million "National Construction Service Program." The program, which was begun early in 1961, called for various public work projects, including highway and dam construction, irrigation, flood control, and reforestation.[2] In February the United States concluded several new agreements with Dr. Chang, covering American economic, technical and related assistance. These actions followed his agreement to revise the hwan-dollar rate of exchange to a more realistic level.

Unfortunately for the Democratic regime, neither the public works projects nor the other programs it initiated were able to bring about any immediate improvements in South Korea's economic situation. As a consequence the mood of the people, which had been one of great hopes and expectations the previous summer, turned against the government. "The Koreans expected all their troubles to be straightened out after Rhee," General Magruder remarked. "They haven't been, and the people are impatient for an improvement in their standard of living." [3]

Premier Chang found himself handicapped not only by South Korea's economic troubles, but also by a turbulent political situation. In a few short months following Rhee's departure, the number of newspapers and periodicals in the country rose from 592 to nearly 1,500 with many of them serving the interests of "numberless warring political factions, groups, cabals, and sub-groups." Even within the

2 "The National Construction Service Program," *Korean Report,* Vol. 1, No. 1 (April 1961), pp. 7-10.
3 *The New York Times,* February 9, 1961.

Democratic party disputes broke out over the government's programs. Amid a general feeling of liberation
from restraints of the past, the country witnessed a heady
political and press freedom that bordered on anarchy.

It was not very long before Chang's desk was piled with
complaints and criticism about unemployment, food shortages and general lack of economic progress. By March
1961 these complaints led to new mass demonstrations in
several Korean cities demanding his resignation. The possibility of another "April revolution" began to haunt the
government, and reports circulated in Seoul that Chang
might "go the way of Syngman Rhee." [4] In a radio broadcast from North Korea, the Communists—reporting with
satisfaction the deteriorating situation in the south—predicted there soon would be a new uprising "by the people."

In May the uprising came, but not the one anticipated.
On May 16, during the early morning hours, a group of
young ROK army officers secretly dispatched 3,000 troops
to the capital and swiftly seized control of the government.
Members of the Chang regime put up no resistance. Most
of them were promptly jailed or placed under house
arrest; the prime minister fled into hiding. To a surprised
nation, the junta announced that it had successfully completed a bloodless coup and declared martial law. Henceforth, it said, the Republic would be ruled by a revolutionary committee—which later was reconstituted as the
"Supreme Council for National Reconstruction."

As to its reasons for the coup, the junta said it had been
forced to act because: (a) the fate of the country and
people could no longer be entrusted "to the corrupt and

[4] *The New York Times,* March 17, 1961; *Los Angeles Times,* April
6, 1961.

incompetent present regime and established politicians";
and (b) it believed that "the time had come to give direction to the nation, which is dangerously astray." [5] The
next day Dr. Chang emerged from hiding to announce
the resignation of his government, and the figurehead
president, Yun Po Sun, also resigned. However, Yun was
persuaded to resume his post several days later, in order to
preserve South Korea's diplomatic ties with the United
States and a dozen other countries.

In spite of the earlier rumors, the overthrow of the
Chang government caught the U.N. Command and the
United States by surprise. The same day of the coup
General Magruder demanded that the chiefs of the Korean
armed forces "use their authority and influence to see
that control is immediately turned back to the lawful
government authorities and that order is restored to the
armed forces." [6] The U.S. chargé d'affaires in Seoul, Marshall Green, concurred, declaring that the United States
continued to support "the constitutional Government of
the Republic of Korea as elected by the people last July
and as constituted last August with the election of a
Prime Minister." [7]

In response to these demands and declarations, the
junta prepared a letter of explanation for the new American President, John F. Kennedy. Signed by Lt. Gen. Chang
Do Young, the nominal head of the revolutionaries, the
letter assured Kennedy that the junta was fully committed
to upholding "democracy, based on liberty." However, the
junta argued that the country's economic and political
situation had been deteriorating and that it had acted

[5] *The New York Times,* May 17, 1961.
[6] *A Historical Summary of United States-Korean Relations,* p. 135.
[7] *Ibid.*

in order to ward off "Communist threats." It pledged the
junta would continue to support South Korea's international commitments, and promised to "hand over the
control of the government to clean and conscientious
civilians . . . and return to proper duties of the military"
after it had strengthened the country.[8]

The United States made no immediate response. As the
days passed, however, and it became clear that the junta
was in effective control, the Americans had little choice
but to recognize the military regime. On May 26, in a
statement issued in Seoul, the U.S. acknowledged receipt
of the junta's letter, and noted with approval its pledge
to eventually return the country to civilian control. Almost
simultaneously the U.S. began a campaign to bring about
a return of civilian government. Thus, for example, on
July 4, 1961 the newly-arrived U.S. ambassador, Samuel
D. Berger, pointedly praised President Yun Po Sun—the
last remaining elected official in the government—as "the
symbol of the new hopes and aspirations of the Korean
people." [9]

The same day Berger was making clear Washington's attitude, the leadership of the junta formally changed hands
as Major General Park Chung Hee stepped forward as
chairman of the Supreme Council for National Reconstruction. Park was identified as a one-time school teacher
who had begun his military career in the Japanese army.
An official biography, released by the junta after he took
over, described him as the youngest of seven children born
into a farm family. Short and slight of build, he grew up
"a quiet, self-possessed lad who seldom laughed." [10] His

[8] *Korean Report,* Vol. 1, No. 2 (June 1961), p. 21.
[9] *Philadelphia Inquirer,* July 5, 1961.
[10] *Korean Report,* Vol. 1, No. 4 (October 1961), pp. 9-10.

sober visage as he took over the military regime at the age of 45 showed he had changed little from the days of his youth.

Following World War II service with the Japanese army in China, Park returned to Korea and joined the South Korean Constabulary. However, in 1948 his military career almost came to an end when he was court martialed and sentenced to death for participating in a Communist-led uprising at Yosu in Chollo-Namdo province.* According to Park's later explanation of this mysterious incident (which his official biography failed to mention), he was implicated for harboring friends of his brother, who were suspected Communists.[11] He was pardoned, however, after fellow officers interceded on his behalf. Later, during the Korean war, he served honorably and rose to the rank of brigadier general. He was then 36. In 1953 he attended a U.S. army artillery school at Fort Sill, Oklahoma and on his return to Korea served in a number of important army posts. At the time of his coup, he was deputy commander of the ROK Second army.

In late May 1961, before Park stepped forward as the junta's leader, the military men embarked on a vigorous campaign to rid South Korea of "subversive" and "corrupt" influences. Within weeks they had arrested more than 13,300 persons, including hoodlums, black marketeers, and several thousand "Communist and pro-Communist agents." [12] A number of the accused Communists were executed. In addition, they jailed a number of former government officials, businessmen, and military men on charges of enriching themselves at the expense of the na-

* See page 86.

[11] *The New York Herald Tribune,* July 4, 1961.

[12] The Secretariat, Supreme Council for National Reconstruction, *Military Revolution in Korea* (Seoul: November 5, 1961), p. 81.

tion. They also indicated 440 procurers, and ordered 4,411 prostitutes returned to their homes.[13]

These mailed fist tactics quickly cowed all opposition in the country, and by early summer General Park and his military advisers were free to turn their attention to South Korea's still unresolved economic problems. They had little difficulty grasping the basic dilemma facing their amputated country. In their own words, South Korea was economically "backward," hampered by "an enormous number of illiterates, unemployment, extreme poverty, shortage of resources," and similar weaknesses.[14] Under these unfavorable conditions, they argued that a democratic form of government was difficult to achieve "without first realizing economic development." Economic progress, however, depended on an injection of a great amount of national capital which South Korea had never possessed.

The Park regime had become aware, as had the governments before it, that the resources available to it were extremely limited. One possible solution was to seek more assistance from the United States. However, Washington had already poured more than $3 billion into the country in economic and technical aid, and since 1957 had been gradually reducing the amounts provided each year. Another possibility was for South Korea to restore economic and political ties with Japan, a policy which the United States had been urging for almost a decade.*

In July the military regime queried the United States about further aid credits. Washington indicated it was

<hr />

13 *The New York Times*, May 29, 1961.

14 *Military Revolution in Korea*, p. 225.

* ROK-Japanese "normalization" talks were pursued intermittently but without results, during the Rhee era. Under Dr. Chang, the negotiations were continued and led to some easing of relations, although formal ties were not restored.

agreeable; however, it lay down two conditions for such assistance: (a) that the regime release the arrested civilian leaders, and (b) that General Park make a specific commitment to return the government to civilian control. In this regard, the junta also was under simultaneous pressure from the United Nations commission on the unification and rehabilitation of Korea (UNCURK). This Korean-based agency, soon after the coup, expressed the hope that civil liberties and democratic government would be quickly restored.[15] Its views, like those of the United States, could not be ignored by the junta without endangering South Korea's international position.

On August 12, 1961, in response to these various economic and political pressures, General Park announced that the Supreme Council would return the government to civilian control in the summer of 1963.[16] Following this announcement, he ordered the release of thousands of prisoners, and also later dropped charges against former members of the Chang government. These actions satisfied the Americans and led, in September, to a formal invitation to Park to visit President Kennedy in Washington.

In preparation for this visit, Secretary of State Dean Rusk flew to Korea in early November for a brief meeting with Park and other South Korean officials. On his departure for Japan, Rusk praised the Park government and declared that the United States expected to continue military and economic aid to the Republic. A few days later Park embarked on his American journey, stopping off in Tokyo for a one-day conference with Japanese officials on renewal of diplomatic and economic ties between the two countries.

15 *The New York Times*, June 13, 1961.
16 *Korean Report*, Vol. 1, No. 4 (October 1961), p. 2.

On November 14 the Korean general was in Washington where he met President Kennedy for "a friendly and constructive exchange of views on the current situation in Korea and the Far East." The two leaders afterwards issued a joint communique in which the President pledged to provide "all possible economic aid" to South Korea, and General Park reiterated the "solemn pledges of the Revolutionary government to return the government to civilian control in the summer of 1963." Kennedy expressed his satisfaction with this pledge "to restore civilian government at the earliest possible date." [17]

In the months that followed, the Park regime inaugurated an ambitious five-year economic development program, instituted various measures to stimulate the country's industrial growth, and greatly expanded South Korea's diplomatic relations with other countries.* These and other economic reforms had a positive effect. During 1962 Korean exports rose substantially as increased production was achieved in the coutry's coal, copper, lead mining, and textile industries. So noteworthy were the improvements compared to earlier years that one American aid official voiced the opinion that the Park regime was "the best Korean government since liberation . . ." [18] However, many basic economic weaknesses had not been resolved, including large-scale unemployment, shortages of skilled labor, a continuing high rate of population growth, and the nation's heavy dependence on American assistance.

[17] *The New York Times*, November 16, 1961.

* By August 1963 South Korea had established some form of diplomatic relations with 53 countries—four times the number that existed prior to 1961.

[18] *Ibid.*, May 28, 1962.

In the political arena during this period the Park regime remained undemocratic and dictatorial. For example, in March 1962 it drafted a "Political Activities Purification Act" which barred more than 4,363 civilians from future political activity. In protest at the promulgation of this political blacklist, President Yun Po Sun resigned from his office. Whereupon, Park assumed the title of acting president as well as chairman of the council. On May 30, however, following a general screening, the Council "cleared" the names of 1,336 politicians for participation in future elections.

Despite the above, criticism of the Park regime remained mute during 1962, as the country awaited the promised changeover to civilian control. In a first step towards that goal, the council in December 1962 completed a draft of a new constitution for the Republic.* Emphasizing a strong executive, it called for: (a) election of a president for a four-year term; (b) strong presidential powers including the right to appoint and dismiss the premier and cabinet members without legislative consent; and (c) establishment of a weak unicameral legislature. On December 19 the constitution was submitted to a national referendum and was approved by 78.8 percent of the voters.

The people's ratification of the constitution greatly encouraged the Park government, but it also set into motion six months of political instability. The new "time of troubles" began on December 27 when General Park announced that members of the Supreme Council "wishing to do so" would run in the forthcoming elections. These men, he said, would retire from the armed services. He also announced that he planned to join the political party

---

*A Harvard University professor of government, Rupert Emerson, served as an advisor to the Council during the drafting of the constitution.

they would form, and would run for president in the elections in April 1963.

Following this announcement and after the civilian politicians were authorized to renew their activity, a group of opposition parties formed in January 1963 and embarked on a campaign against the military regime. These parties charged the Council with reneging on its pledge to return to army duties after the transfer of power. They also denounced the Political Purification Law, demanded that Park not run for the presidency, and asked that the elections be postponed in order to allow them time to complete their party organization.[19]

Although Park had expected some criticism of the regime, what he had not expected was an outbreak of a feud within the Supreme Council itself. The internal dissension arose in late January after the formation of the junta-backed Democratic Republican party, Park's vehicle for his campaign for the presidency. Differences arose over the makeup of the party, and its control by Brig. Gen. Kim Chong Pil, one of the young "architects" of the 1961 coup, and head of the Korean Central Intelligence Agency. As the dispute raged, several Council members resigned in protest, and Park dispatched Kim overseas as an "ambassador at large." *

The major consequences of this internal disorder was a great loss of prestige for the Council and General Park. From the moment he had stepped forward as leader of the military government, Park had denounced the civilian

[19] *Report of the United Nations Commission on the Unification and Rehabilitation of Korea*, General Assembly, Official Records: Eighteenth Session, Supplement No. 12 (A/551 2), p. 11.

* Kim, who was related to Park by marriage, was subsequently restored as head of the Democratic Republican party. In the spring of 1964, however, student unrest directed against him forced Park to send Kim into a new "exile."

politicians who had preceded him for their factionalism feuds. Now the events of January 1963 showed his own group was not immune to such jealousies and maneuverings for power. In apparent disgust and anger, Park announced on February 18 that he would not participate in any future government—if the civilian leaders would take certain pledges to ensure future stability. In late February, during a special ceremony in Seoul, all major parties accepted Park's proposals.

The general's decision to step aside proved, however, to be transient. By mid-March he had overcome his personal chagrin and, with the elections fast approaching, he also changed his mind about proceeding with the turnover of the government to the civilians. On March 16, following an announcement of a "plot" to overthrow the Council, Park said he had decided to extend military rule for four more years and would submit the proposal to another national referendum. Simultaneously, he banned all political activity and speeches "of a political nature," and partially restricted freedom of assembly and freedom of the press.

This startling decision raised a great storm of protest throughout South Korea. Former acting premier Huh Chung denounced Park's reversal as "a major tragedy for the Korean people." Yun Po Sun also was highly critical, and accused the general of destroying "the democracy which had just begun budding." Together with other civilian leaders, they demanded that Park withdraw his proposal; to emphasize their opposition, they undertook "silent marches" through the streets of Seoul.

The United States was as dismayed by this turn of events as were the civilian leaders. In the days that followed,

[20] *The New York Times*, March 16, 1963.

while Washington remained silent Ambassador Berger and other U. S. officials in Seoul sought to persuade the general and the Council to return to their original election plan. On March 25 the U. S. issued its first public statement on the crisis, warning that "prolongation of military rule could constitute a threat to stable and effective government." On April 2, 1963 President Kennedy, urging the early transfer of power to the civilians, expressed America's firm opposition to the perpetuation of an unconstitutional government.[21]

Park and the Council faced a major crisis. It was much too late to restore the junta's unchallenged rule, since reverting to force would lose it the support of the U. S. and the U. N. and create dangerous internal dissensions. In early April, after much backing and filling, Park finally agreed to allow a resumption of political life. Several weeks later he reaffirmed his intention to restore power to a civilian government, and followed this with an announcement that free elections would be held in the fall. Thus six months of political instability came to an end, and the United States received great credit for the favorable outcome of the crisis.[22]

The election campaign for the third Republic of Korea began during the late summer months of 1963, with a half-dozen parties participating. Besides Park's Democratic Republican party,* the other competing groups included the Civil Rule party, the Democratic party, the Party of the People, and the Liberal Democratic party. Former president Yun Po Sun, nominated as the candidate of the

21 *Ibid.*, April 3, 1963.

22 *Ibid.*, April 8, 1963.

* In order to participate in the election, Park resigned from the army on August 30.

Civil Rule party, soon emerged as Park's strongest opponent for the presidency.

Following an intensive campaign, during which Yun charged that Park had once been a Communist (referring to the Yosu incident of 1948), the elections were held on October 15 and proved to be the most honest ever held in the country. When the results were tabulated, Park had edged out Yun by a vote of 4,702,640 to 4,546,613. U. N. observers testified to the fairness of the balloting.

Six weeks later—while the president-elect was in Washington attending the funeral of President Kennedy—* Park's Democratic Republican party achieved a notable victory in the National Assembly elections. It won control of 110 of the 175 seats,[23] while Yun's party won 41 seats to emerge as the largest opposition party. Several members of the junta won their races for seats in the legislature, including Kim Chong Pil and retired general Chang Kyun Doon.

On December 17 Park took the formal oath of office as president of the third Republic, and urged his countrymen to "throw off the yoke of backwardness." He pledged his regime would seek to establish "a strong economic and social foundation," would act "with efficiency and dispatch" to solve the country's economic woes, and would strengthen its ties "with the United Nations and all of the freedom loving peoples of the world."

Thus by the end of 1963 the new strongman of South Korea emerged, with sufficient parliamentary support to carry out his plans of "giving direction to the nation," but still facing great economic and social problems and a

* Park met briefly with President Lyndon B. Johnson following Kennedy's funeral on November 25, and was assured of continued American interest and support of South Korea.

23 *Korean Report,* Vol. 3, No. 7 (October-November 1963), p. 4.

restive, unhappy younger generation. During all these political events the old Korean strongman, Syngman Rhee, lay ill and worn in a nursing home in Hawaii, his days of power and glory behind him.

# 17

## The Continuing Korean Cold War
## and the Sino-Soviet Dispute

WHILE political power was passing from the hands of Rhee to Chang to Park, the cold war over Korea continued its obstinate course at Panmunjom. Rhee had exaggerated only slightly when he charged the Communists had broken the armistice agreement "even before the ink was dry." Within twenty-four hours after the fighting ended on July 27, 1953, they flew new Soviet combat aircraft into northern bases. This action was in direct violation of provisions of the agreement prohibiting introduction of reinforcing personnel or equipment. It was, however, only the beginning of such violations, by which the Communists rebuilt the shattered military forces of North Korea.

Through its intelligence agencies the United States quickly learned of the new military activity in the north, and it promptly protested to the Communist members of the Military Armistice Commission at Panmunjom. The Chinese and North Koreans, however, denied all accusations, and instead charged the Americans themselves with breaking the armistice. Washington, although unhappy over the violations, kept its eye mainly on the ceasefire which it was convinced would be observed by the Communists.

The American government's belief that there would be a long armistice and stalemate was based on the warning

217

issued by the sixteen nations of the U.N. Command, which in effect stated there would be no privileged sanctuaries in a second Korean war, and on intimations from President Eisenhower that the U.S. would resort to nuclear weapons should the Communists renew their attack.[1]

United States policy during the first years of the armistice thus was to maintain the status quo along the truce line. This involved, in the military sphere, support of two American army divisions, the 500,000-man ROK army, and token United Nations units. But as the years passed and the Communist buildup continued, the balance of military forces in the peninsula began to change and threatened to finally shift against the U.N. side. North Korea's air strength, for example, rose from zero in 1953 to some 700 aircraft, mostly Soviet jet fighters, in 1957. The Communists also introduced artillery pieces in the 122mm. mortars, and the 75/76 howitzer.[2]

By 1957 defense officials in Washington and Seoul had become concerned over the possibility that the Communists might, on the basis of their new military power, again miscalculate American intentions. Whereupon, in the spring of that year the U.S. undertook a review of its military policy towards Korea and decided, as a precautionary measure, to reinforce U.N. forces in the peninsula. On July 21 the Americans announced their plan in advance to the Communists, assuring them, however, that the U.N. side would continue to abide by the ceasefire.[3] The reinforcements which followed this announcement included not only new American jet aircraft, but also army missile units "with atomic capability."

[1] Dwight D. Eisenhower, *Mandate for Change, 1953-1956*, Vol. I, The White House Years (New York: Doubleday, 1963), pp. 180, 248.

[2] State Department, *The Record of Korean Unification, 1943-1960* (Washington: Government Printing Office, 1960), p. 208.

[3] *Ibid.*, p. 209.

The Communists promptly and vigorously denounced the U.S. plan, and initiated an angry worldwide propaganda campaign against it. However, it was obvious to both sides that neither had the power to prevent the other from doing what it pleased in its own areas. The original Korean armistice agreement as such was dead. All that remained was a de facto ceasefire, and two hostile armies dug in on both sides of the armistice line. During the years that followed these events, the Military Armistice Commission continued to meet at Panmunjom, where charges of violations and cold war vituperation marked the useless proceedings.*

In the immediate post-war years, while the Communists were rebuilding their North Korean forces, they also embarked on a persistent campaign to bring about a new political conference. Despite the failure of the Geneva conference, the Pyongyang regime in November 1954 and again in March 1955 appealed to the South Koreans to join them in new political talks on Korea. General Nam Il, the Communist foreign minister, offered to meet with ROK representatives at Panmunjom or Kaesong to discuss political, cultural and economic questions. "Let the Koreans," he said, "sit around one table by themselves, and let Americans pull out of Korea." [4] However, after Geneva Rhee had said: "Future talks are hopeless, whether they are held at Panmunjom, Geneva, or heaven itself." [5]

The Communists renewed their call for a conference in 1956 and 1957. In the spring of 1956 it was Peiping which proposed to meet with the U.N. side "to discuss the question of the withdrawal from Korea of all foreign troops

* During the first ten years of the armistice (August 1953 to August 1963), a total of 177 full Commission meetings were held.

[4] *Tokyo Mainichi*, November 1, 1954; *Nippon Times*, March 11, 1955.
[5] *The New York Times*, August 1, 1954.

and of the peaceful unification of Korea." [6] However, when the Chinese rejected a U.N. counter proposal that they agree on the principle of U.N.-supervised elections in Korea, this proposal and a similar 1957 offer lapsed.

In early 1958 the North Koreans opened the campaign with the most ambitious Communist effort to that time. On February 5 Radio Pyongyang broadcast a detailed proposal to the U.N. side, calling for: (a) the simultaneous withdrawal from Korea of the "U.S. army and all other foreign troops including the Chinese People's Volunteers"; (b) the holding of "all-Korea free elections" to be observed by a "neutral nations" organization; (c) direct negotiations between Seoul and Pyongyang on economic and cultural matters; and (d) reduction of the sizes of the armies in both north and south.

The Soviets and Chinese quickly gave their endorsement to the North Korean proposal. On February 7, in a communication to the U.N. side, the Chinese announced that "in order to break the deadlock on the Korean question," they were prepared to pull their troops from Korea.[7] They again called for a political conference to discuss the withdrawal of all non-Korean troops and the overall problem of unification. Without waiting for the western response, the Chinese dispatched Premier Chou En-lai to Pyongyang where, on February 19, he and North Korean Premier Kim Il Sung signed a formal agreement for withdrawal of the Chinese armies.[8] The evacuation of Peiping's forces followed soon thereafter, and was reported completed eight months later.

This Communist strategem took place almost exactly on the tenth anniversary of a similar withdrawal of Rus-

[6] *Ibid.,* June 1, 1956.
[7] *The Record of Korean Unification, 1943-1960,* p. 214-216.
[8] *Supplement to New Korea,* No. 3 (Pyongyang), March 1958, pp. 2-5.

sian troops from North Korea in 1948. However, where before the United States had eagerly seized the opportunity to evacuate its own forces, and soon regretted the decision, it had no intention of making the same mistake again. On April 9, through the offices of the British government, Washington informed the Chinese of its pleasure at learning of the North Korean plan to hold free elections observed by a neutral nations organization, and of the Chinese troop withdrawal. However, it asked Peiping for clarification of the several proposals, and whether the Communist side agreed that free elections "should be held under United Nations auspices" with adequate supervision both before and during the balloting.[9]

This note, which avoided the issue of troop withdrawal, angered the Chinese, who now accused the U.S. of "an obvious attempt to divert the attention of the peoples of the world." In a new communication dated May 8, Peiping insisted on knowing "when the Governments of the United States and the other countries on the United Nations Command side intend to withdraw all their forces from South Korea." [10] Washington's response, in the name of its U.N. allies, was forwarded to Peiping on July 2. "United Nations forces," the U.S. informed the Chinese, "are in Korea at the instance of the United Nations. In accordance with the existing recommendations of the General Assembly of the United Nations, the Governments concerned are prepared to withdraw their forces from Korea when the conditions for a lasting settlement laid down by the General Assembly have been fulfilled." [11]

These conditions, however, continued to be anathema to the Communists. On November 10 the Chinese declared

[9] *The Record of Korean Unification, 1943-1960* pp. 216-217.
[10] *Ibid.,* pp. 218-220.
[11] *Ibid.,* p. 221.

that they would never accept free elections in Korea under United Nations supervision. The international organization, they charged, "under the domination of the United States," has been reduced to "a belligerent in the Korean war and lost all competence and moral authority to deal fairly and reasonably with the Korean question." [12]

The Communist-initiated dialogue lapsed for more than a year—until 1960 when Rhee's ouster from power in Seoul appeared to offer a new opportunity for achieving the goal of a Korea united under Communist control. On August 15—on the fifteenth anniversary of Korea's liberation from Japan—Kim Il Sung called upon Rhee's successors to join with him in the creation of a "Korean federation." Such a federation, he said, could be preceded by a general election "held throughout the north and south without any influence by foreign nations." The North Korean leader suggested that the two regimes take immediate steps to establish "a supreme national committee" which would undertake economic and cultural exchanges.

Kim's seductive proposal was seconded by Soviet Premier Nikita S. Khrushchev during an address to the U. N. General Assembly on September 25, 1960. The leader of the Soviet Union—speaking a little over ten years after Moscow initiated the Korean war—argued that "only madmen can contemplate solving the Korean question through the use of armed force." The only correct solution, Khrushchev said, was to leave the question of Korea's reunification "to the Koreans," with the necessary condition for that being "the immediate and complete withdrawal of all American troops from South Korea, whose presence poisons the atmosphere. . . ." [13]

[12] *Ibid.*, pp. 223-225.
[13] *The New York Times*, September 26, 1960.

This latest Communist effort to get U.S. troops out of the peninsula and to obtain direct negotiations with the South Koreans was rejected by the United States and the Seoul government. However, in an effort to demonstrate some flexibility, the South Korean Assembly on November 2 discarded the old Rhee position that elections be held only in North Korea. For the first time it offered to accept U.N.-sponsored elections throughout the entire country. This initiative, however, was wasted. As before, the Communists refused to recognize the competence or annual resolutions of the United Nations,* well aware that such "outside interference in the internal affairs of the Korean people" would mean the end of their power in the country.

After nearly twenty years of hot and cold war, the division of Korea seemed irrevocable. Yet there was something new in the total political equation in Asia—a shifting of allegiances arising from the historic Sino-Soviet dispute which, beginning in 1960, slowly began to affect the orientation of the North Korean government.

The Moscow-Peiping controversy began four years earlier at the twentieth Soviet party congress, when Premier Khrushchev denounced the tyrannical rule of Stalin, and announced Moscow's full commitment to the policy of "peaceful coexistence." The government of Mao Tse-tung became convinced, especially after the Polish and Hungarian uprisings in October-November 1956, that both Soviet actions were a mistake, and would harm the Communist cause throughout the world.[14] Chinese criticism,

* On December 13, 1963 the General Assembly, as it had done almost every year since the armistice, reaffirmed the objective of bringing about the establishment of a unified, independent, and democratic Korea, and called upon the Communists to accept these goals.

[14] See Donald S. Zagoria, *The Sino-Soviet Conflict, 1956-1961* (Princeton University Press, 1962); Edward Chankshaw, *The New Cold War: Moscow v. Pekin* (New York: Penguin, 1963).

however, did not take on a sharp edge until the summer of 1959, after the Soviet Union unilaterally abrograted an agreement it had signed 21 months earlier with Mao to help China acquire nuclear weapons.[15] When the Chinese stepped up their criticism of Moscow's policies, the Soviet Union in July-August 1960 drastically reduced its economic and technical aid to Peiping. The Chinese reacted to this "unfriendly" move by violating the Soviet-Sinkiang border more than 5,000 times (according to Moscow) and by attempting to "develop" Soviet territory "without permission."[16] These events led to Chinese-Soviet armed clashes along the long frontier.

This remarkable falling-out of the Chinese and Russians soon began to have repercussions throughout the Communist world, including in North Korea. For the Pyongyang regime, it opened up a particularly difficult period. A creature of the Soviet Union, it originally was entirely subservient to Moscow, being dominated by a special elite composed of Soviet citizens of Korean descent, recruited from Korean communities in the Soviet Union. According to the U.S. State Department, these Soviet-Koreans "retained their Soviet citizenship and generally remained in the background in the North Korean political arena, but they were infiltrated into, and dominated, the top levels of the party and the government."[17]

Premier Kim Il Sung himself, the very model of a Communist satellite leader, had entered North Korea in August 1945 as a captain in the Soviet army. His basic allegiance to the Soviet Union apparently remained stead-

[15] *The New York Times*, September 14, 1963.

[16] An official Soviet government statement referring to these incidents was published in *Izvestia*, with excerpts reprinted in *The New York Times*, September 23, 1963.

[17] State Department, *North Korea: A Case Study in the Techniques of Takeover* (Washington: Government Printing Office, 1961), p. 5.

fast despite the debacle of the Korean war, or the massive Chinese Communist intervention.* Indeed, both before and after the war, the Chinese continued to recognize, or made no effort to challenge, Russia's domination of North Korea.[18] Nevertheless, the presence of large continents of Chinese troops in the country between 1951 and 1958 seems to have strengthened the position of the so-called "Yenan" faction of Koreans, some of whom had previously lived in Chinese Communist-dominated areas.

Beginning in October 1960—two months after the Soviets cut off their technical and economic assistance to China—Peiping opened a campaign to win over the North Koreans. In an action which amounted to a thumbing of its nose at Moscow, it signed its own economic assistance program with Pyongyang—a $105 million program spread over a four-year period. Under its provisions, Peiping agreed to help furnish equipment for North Korea's tire, radio, cotton and other light industries, and promised to send Chinese technicians to help with training.[19]

The signing of the Sino-North Korean pact was Mao's declaration of independence from the Soviet Union. It also signalled the opening of a tug-of-war for North Korea's allegiance. In late May 1961 Moscow sought to recoup by sending First Deputy Premier A. N. Kosygin to Pyongyang to "reassure" the North Koreans of continuing Soviet support in the face of the military revolt in Seoul. The Kosygin visit gave the Russians the opportunity to woo Kim Il Sung, and to invite him to Moscow

---

* According to Lt. Col. Yuri A. Rastvorov, a Soviet defectee, Stalin negotiated with Mao for Chinese military intervention after U.N. troops began their advance into North Korea. See Rastvorov, "Red Fraud and Intrigue in the Far East," *Life,* Vol. 37 (December 5, 1954), p. 175.

[18] Maurice Chanteloup, "Moscow, Not Peking, Still Drives North Korea," *Tokyo Mainichi,* October 2, 1953.

[19] *Los Angeles Times,* October 20, 1960.

where he was offered a formal 10-year Soviet military assistance treaty (signed on July 6).[20] During his Russian visit Kim was praised highly by Khrushchev, and later he joined in a Soviet communique which denounced "deviations from the socialist internationalism" [21]—a direct attack on Peiping's anti-Moscow activities.

From the Soviet Union, however, Kim flew directly to Peiping where he also was presented with a Chinese treaty of friendship, cooperation and mutual assistance. Kim lingered afterwards in China for conversations with Mao, whom he had previously met in December 1958, and on his departure he signed another joint communique in which both leaders declared that the chief danger to world communism was Yugoslav (Soviet) "revisionism." [22] Thus, in the space of three weeks, Kim managed to parrot the lines of both Moscow and Peiping.

This extraordinary effort to straddle the Sino-Soviet dispute continued throughout the latter half of 1961. However, Kim was under great pressure from the pro-Chinese faction in his party, and at the twenty-second Soviet party congress held in Moscow in October, he sided with Peiping in refusing to condemn the anti-Khrushchevian Albanians. On his return to North Korea, however, Kim expressed "deep concern" over the Albanian issue. Trying desperately to avoid making a final choice, he pledged that the Korean people would "always march" with the Soviets, while, however, strengthening their "militant friendship and solidarity with the Chinese Communist party. . . . " [23]

20 *The New York Times,* July 7, 1961.

21 Zagoria, *op. cit.,* p. 380.

22 *The New York Times,* July 21, 1961.

23 Alexander Dallin, ed. *Diversity in International Communism: A Documentary Record, 1961-1963* (New York: Columbia University Press, 1963), pp. 288-394.

Kim's ambivalent attitude could not long be maintained in the face of the Chinese campaign to end Pyongyang's dependence on Moscow. Thus, towards the end of April 1962, Peiping dispatched a large Chinese delegation to North Korea led by Peng Chen, representing the National People's Congress. The Chinese stayed for three weeks. In mid-June a delegation from the North Korean Supreme Peoples Assembly paid a return visit to China. The statements of both groups showed a growing identity of interests as both again denounced Moscow's policies, i.e., revisionism.

Early in November 1962, in a speech which reflected an intense intra-party struggle by the Soviet-Koreans to return the regime to the Russian fold, Kim aligned himself with the surging Chinese faction by criticizing the "subversive" activities of the "revisionists." [24] His position, however, still remained equivocal, and in the weeks and months that followed the names of other North Korean leaders began to achieve unusual prominence. Thus, for example, in early December, at a meeting of the Czechoslovakia Communist party, it was Vice Premier Lee Chu-yon who again proclaimed North Korea's "solidarity with the Chinese Communist party." [25]

Six months later, in June 1963, President Choe Yong Kon, the titular head of the North Korean regime, embarked on an 18-day state visit to China and proceeded to attack "all aspects of revisionism." Prior to his departure on June 24, Choe signed a joint declaration with the Chinese denouncing Soviet policy and calling on the Communist nations to "strengthen their national defenses, including the development of nuclear superiority." [26] In

[24] *The New York Times*, November 4, 1962.
[25] Dallin, *op. cit.*, pp. 663-664.
[26] *The New York Times*, June 24, 1963.

September Liu Shao-chi, the president of Communist China, made a short return visit to North Korea and praised the local party as Peiping's "close comrade in arms." The two countries once more reaffirmed their "complete identity of views." [27]

North Korea's pro-Chinese orientation was not without significance for the United States, South Korea and the free world. During its dispute with Moscow, Peiping consistently derided the Soviet policy of "peaceful coexistence," and urged Communists and "suppressed peoples" throughout the world to become more militant in an armed struggle against "the imperialists." In Latin America, Africa and Southeast Asia, the Chinese gave encourgement to various insurrectionist movements.

In North Korea, which politically at least seemed to have foresaken Moscow,* the regime answered Peiping's call to action by initiating a series of armed clashes along the truce line in late July and August 1963. They resulted in new Korean and American casualties including a half-dozen new deaths. The flareup of fighting between patrols of both sides was a reminder to the world that the struggle for Korea had not ended, and that a solution to the Korean problem remained as elusive as ever.

---

[27] *Ibid.*, September 19, 1963.

* Militarily, the North Koreans remained almost entirely dependent on the Soviet Union since their armed forces were equipped with Russian planes, tanks, artillery, etc. This circumstance made it difficult for Pyongyang to break with Moscow.

# 18

## Conclusion

TODAY WE AND the Russians, Koreans and Chinese cannot escape from the consequences of the blunders commited in Korea by the United States and the Soviet Union. As we have seen, neither Moscow nor Washington originally had any intention of permanently dividing Korea, yet their hurried decisions made during the climax of World War II produced that disastrous event. Neither did the United States intend to encourage a Communist invasion of South Korea when it withdrew its occupation forces in 1949, nor did the Soviet Union expect U.S. interference when it launched the 1950 aggression to unify the peninsula by force. These and other gross miscalculations by both sides mock the efforts of the great powers to anticipate, much less to control, the course of political or military events.

The irony of the Korean tragedy, however, is that from the errors and misjudgments that were made, many positive events have followed which, in the long run, may be more important than the division of that country. For example, it is clear that the Communist invasion of South Korea, and the United States intervention, were major turning points in the cold war. It is no coincidence that Korea remains today as the only place in Europe or Asia where the Soviet Union since 1945 resorted to overt military action to expand the territories under its control.

For this blessing, we must pay homage to President Truman. Winston Churchill described Truman's action in Korea as having "turned the fortunes of the free world to sure hope of peace"; that is, it deterred other large-scale Communist aggressions and may have prevented a third world war.

The unexpected American intervention in Korea in June 1950 clearly startled, if not astounded, the leaders of the Soviet Union. Not only did Truman's action throw Moscow's plans into turmoil, but it threatened a direct Soviet-American clash. Determined to avoid war with the United States at all costs, Stalin called upon Mao for troop assistance. Following the armistice, his successors backed away even further from Korean-like adventures, resurrecting an old Communist slogan called "peaceful coexistence," * which they made the foundation of their new foreign policy.

The Soviets' fervidly-proclaimed commitment to peaceful coexistence became even more rational after the United States helped to rearm the nations of Western Europe and, at the same time, undertook to develop a huge American strategic striking force. By 1961 this force included nuclear-tipped intercontinental and submarine ballistic missiles, capable of reaching any point in the Soviet Union. Moscow's caution in the face of this enormous American military power, which it itself had called forth, and Khrushchev's reiteration of the theme of peaceful coexistence, became important factors leading to the breakdown

---

* On December 18, 1925, in a report to the fourteenth Soviet party Congress, Stalin first spoke of the existence of "a certain temporary equilibrium of forces and a certain period of 'peaceful coexistence' between the bourgeois world and the proletarian world." On August 8, 1953—twelve days after the Korean ceasefire—his successor and short-lived Premier, G. M. Malenkov, spoke of the need for reducing international tensions and for "peaceful coexistence."

of Sino-Soviet relations. Because of these Russian policies, according to Mao, the Soviet leaders have become "the chief representatives of modern revisionism as well as the greatest splitters in the international Communist movement."

The great post-1950 rise in American military strength, it should be noted, was a consequence of an historic change in U.S. defense policy resulting largely from the Korean war. The traditional impulse of America previously had been to reduce its peacetime military expenditures to an absolute minimum. Thus, after all of its wars prior to 1950, the United States sought to expeditiously disarm itself. The most spectacular example of this, which was, however, aborted by events, occurred following World War II when the government discharged more than 9.5 million servicemen in a nine-month period.

But even while the American people were embarked on the destruction of their military forces in 1945-1947, their tradition of "free" peacetime security had come to an end, subverted by modern science and technology and the rise of the cold war. The nation's awakening came in a series of shocks, as the Soviets clamped an iron ring around Eastern Europe, stimulated Communist guerrilla action in Greece, overthrew the democratic government of Czechoslovakia, and initiated the Berlin blockade. These actions led to American counter-action, including the adoption of the Truman doctrine (1947), the Marshall plan (1948), the Berlin airlift (1948-1949), and creation of the North Atlantic Treaty Organization (1949). When in the summer of 1949 the Soviet Union exploded its first atomic bomb, the bells had already tolled the passage of American free security.

However, it was not until the Soviets struck in Korea,

followed by their desperate call upon the Chinese Communists after MacArthur's brilliant stroke, that a new American policy was formally adopted by President Truman and his Secretary of Defense, George C. Marshall, and backed by the Congress. This new doctrine called for a rapid and orderly build-up of substantial military strength which would be maintained in peacetime "for an indefinite number of years." Unique in American history, this military policy has been continued by the Eisenhower, Kennedy and Johnson administrations. It was this new element of strength, backed by America's determination to fight, which led the Soviet Union to embrace peaceful coexistence and to turn its attention to less dangerous forms of warfare with the West.

The Korean phase of the East-West struggle, which continues in different forms, had other positive effects beyond those we have just described. One of the most significant was its impact on the United Nations. In the words of Trygve Lie, because of the determined stand taken against agression in Korea by the international body, "collective security was enforced for the first time in the whole of human history." The precedent set in Korea, which greatly strengthened the United Nations, has since been invoked in the 1956 Middle East crisis, the Congo in 1960, and in Cyprus in 1964. By its action in Korea, the United Nations may have saved itself the fate of the inert League of Nations.

From the strictly military point of view, the Korean war was, of course, a failure for both sides. Washington's "refusal" to pursue a military victory in Korea was, for many Americans including General MacArthur, difficult to accept, and was attributed to weakness and even to Communist subversion in the government. Truman's decision to recall the famous commander, however, was made less to reassert presidential authority than, in fact, to emphasize America's world-wide responsibilities and its specific orientation towards Europe.

In 1941, after Pearl Harbor, and in 1950, after the North Korean invasion, Europe came first and it does so at this writing. Perhaps, as MacArthur contended, the United States could have won all of North Korea by enlarging the war against China and without precipitating a world conflict. However, that calculated risk was not taken and the reasons are clear: the North Atlantic alliance was, and is, the cornerstone of American foreign policy, and fears were aroused that American involvement in a large-scale Asian war might weaken European defenses, and bring on a third world war.

It is true that the United States for generations has slighted Asia, but that has been because the nations of the East, backward and "primitive," have rarely posed a direct threat to American security. Even today an Asia dominated by Communist China would not pose the kind of threat to the U.S. that would face the nation should Europe fall under the domination of a single expansionist power. However, the world situation is much changed and changing, and in the years ahead the United States must give greater heed to the defenses of those Asian nations whose independence is threatened by the new Communist imperialism.

As for divided Korea itself, the victim of the great East-West clash, there appears to be no solution in sight. Its destiny, and ours, remains inextricably wound up in the world struggle against the Communist powers. If someday, somehow, there should be a happy ending for Korea, as well as for the other nations facing direct or indirect aggression, it will surely be because the American people remained steadfast to the leadership thrust upon them, and specifically because they maintained their military strength, that necessary condition which the leaders of communism find so distasteful.

# Bibliography

## DOCUMENTARY MATERIAL

*Diversity in International Communism: A Documentary Record, 1961-1963.* Alexander Dallin, ed. New York: Columbia University of Press, 1963.

*Documents on American Foreign Relations,* Vol. VII, 1944-1945 and Vol. XII, 1950. Princeton: Princeton University Press for World Peace Foundation, 1947 and 1951.

*Korean-American Relations, Documents Pertaining to the Far Eastern Diplomacy of the United States.* Vol. 1, *The Initial Period, 1883-1886.* George M. McCune and John A. Harrison, eds. Berkeley and Los Angeles: University of California Press, 1951.

*Public Papers of Presidents of the United States, Dwight D. Eisenhower, 1960-1961.* Washington: Government Printing Office, 1961.

*Semiannual Report of the Secretary of Defense, January 1 to June 30, 1950,* Washington: Government Printing Office, 1950.

*Source Materials on Korean Politics and Ideologies.* Donald Tewksbury, ed. New York: Institute of Pacific Relations, 1950.

STATE DEPARTMENT. *Moscow Meeting of Foreign Ministers.* Washington: Government Printing Office, 1946.

———. *Korea 1945 to 1948.* Washington: Government Printing Office, 1948.

———. *United States Relations With China.* Washington: Government Printing Office, 1949.

———. *U.S. Policy in the Korean Crisis.* Washington: Government Printing Office, 1950.

———. *Strengthening the Forces of Freedom, Selected Speeches and Statements by Secretary of State Acheson.* Washington: Government Printing Office, 1950.

———. *Selected Documents on American Foreign Policy.* Washington: Government Printing Office, 1951.

———. *The Conflict in Korea.* Washington: Government Printing Office, 1951.

———. *The Conferences at Malta and Yalta 1945*. Washington: Government Printing Office, 1955.

———. *The Korean Problem at the Geneva Conference, April 26-June 15, 1954*. Washington: Government Printing Office, 1954.

———. *American Foreign Policy, Basic Documents, 1950-1955*, Vol. II. Washington: Government Printing Office, 1957.

———. *The Record of Korean Unification, 1943-1960*. Washington: Government Printing Office, 1960.

*The Letters of Theodore Roosevelt*, Vol. IV, The Square Deal, 1903-1905. Cambridge: Harvard University Press, 1951.

*The Public Papers and Addresses of Franklin D. Roosevelt:* The 1942 Volume. Samuel I. Rosenman, ed. New York: Harper & Brothers, 1942.

*The War Reports of General George C. Marshall, General H. H. Arnold and Fleet Admiral Ernest J. King*. Philadelphia: Lippincott, 1947.

*Transcript of Proceedings of Military Armistice Conference at Kaesong and Panmunjom, Korea, July, 1951 to July, 1953*. General Headquarters UNC (Advance). Documents at Office of Chief of Military History, Washington.

U.S. CONGRESS, SENATE. *The United States and the Korean Problem, Documents 1943-1953*. Washington: Government Printing Office, 1953.

———. *Military Situation in the Far East*. 5 pts. Hearings Before Committee on Armed Services and Committee on Foreign Relations, U.S. Senate, 82d Cong. 1st Sess. on military situation in Far East and the facts surrounding the relief of General Douglas MacArthur. Washington: Government Printing Office, 1951.

———. *Interlocking Subversion in Government Departments*. Hearings Before the Subcommittee to Investigate the Administration of the Internal Security Act and Other Internal Security Act and Other Internal Security Laws of the Committee on the Judiciary, U.S. Senate, 83rd Cong., 2d Sess. Pts. 21, 22, 24, 25, 26. Washington: Government Printing Office, 1954 and 1955.

## BOOKS

*General*

ALLEN, RICHARD. *Korea's Syngman Rhee: An Unauthorized Portrait*. Rutland, Vt.: Charles E. Tuttle, 1960.

BISHOP, ISABELLA BIRD. *Korea and Her Neighbors.* New York: Fleming H. Revell Co., 1897.

CALDWELL, JOHN C. *The Korea Story.* Chicago: Henry Regnery Co., 1952.

CHUNG, HENRY. *The Russians Came to Korea.* Seoul & Washington: Korean Pacific Press, 1947.

CHUNG, KYUNG CHO. *New Korea: New Land of the Morning Calm.* New York: Macmillan, 1962.

CLYDE, PAUL H. *International Rivalries in Manchuria, 1689-1922.* Columbus: Ohio State University Press, 1928.

CRANKSHAW, EDWARD. *The New Cold War: Moscow v. Pekin.* New York: Penguin Books, 1963.

DENNETT, TYLER. *Roosevelt and the Russo-Japanese War.* New York: Doubleday, Page & Co., 1925.

FEIS, HERBERT. *The China Tangle.* Princeton: Princeton University Press, 1955.

FRIEDRICH, CARL L. AND ASSOCIATES. *American Experiences in Military Government in World War II.* New York: Rinehart & Co., 1948.

GEER, ANDREW. *The New Breed, The Story of the U.S. Marines in Korea.* New York: Harper & Brothers, 1952.

GREEN, A. WIGFALL. *The Epic of Korea.* Washington: Public Affairs Press, 1952.

GUNTHER, JOHN. *The Riddle of MacArthur.* New York: Harper & Brothers, 1950.

HULBERT, HOMER B. *The Passing of Korea.* New York: Doubleday, Page & Co., 1906.

KUROPATKIN, ALEXIE N. *The Russian Army and the Japanese War.* A. B. Lindsay, trans. New York: E. P. Dutton & Co., 1909.

MARSHALL, S. L. A. *The River and the Guantlet.* New York: William Morrow & Co., 1953.

MEADE, E. GRANT. *American Military Government in Korea.* New York: King's Crown Press, Columbia Univ., 1951.

McCUNE, GEORGE M. *Korea Today.* Cambridge: Harvard University Press, 1950.

NELSON, M. FREDERICK. *Korea and the Old Order in Eastern Asia.* Baton Rouge: Louisiana State University Press, 1946.

OLIVER, ROBERT T. *Why War Came in Korea.* New York: Fordham University Press, 1950.

——. *Syngman Rhee, The Man Behind the Myth.* New York: Dodd, Mead & Co., 1954.

PYUN, Y. T. *Korea—My Country.* Washington: Korean Pacific Press, 1953.

ROVERE, RICHARD H. & ARTHUR M. SCHLESINGER. *The General and the President.* New York: Farrar, Straus and Young, 1951.

SCHERER, JAMES A. B. *Three Meiji Leaders: Ito, Togo, Nogi.* Tokyo: The Hokuseido Press, 1946.

SHERWOOD, ROBERT E. *Roosevelt and Hopkins, An Intimate History.* New York: Harper & Brothers, 1948.

*South Asia in the World Today.* Phillips Talbott, ed. Chicago: University of Chicago Press, 1951.

SPANIER, JOHN W. *The Truman-MacArthur Controversy and the Korean War.* Cambridge: Belnap Press, 1959.

RHEE, SYNGMAN. *Japan Inside Out.* New York: Fleming H. Revell Co., 1941.

WELLES, SUMNER. *Seven Decisions That Shaped History.* New York: Harper & Brothers, 1950.

ZAGORIA, DONALD S. *The Sino-Soviet Conflict, 1956-1961.* Princeton: Princeton University Press, 1962.

## Memoirs

ADAMS, SHERMAN. *First-Hand Report: The Story of the Eisenhower Administration.* New York: Harper & Brothers, 1961.

BYRNES, JAMES F. *Speaking Frankly.* New York and London: Harper & Brothers, 1947.

CHURCHILL, WINSTON S. *The Gathering Storm.* Boston: Houghton Mifflin Co., 1948.

——. *Their Finest Hour.* Boston: Houghton Mifflin Co., 1949.

——. *The Grand Alliance.* Boston: Houghton Mifflin Co., 1950.

——. *Closing the Ring.* Boston: Houghton Mifflin Co., 1951.

——. *Triumph and Tragedy.* Boston: Houghton Mifflin Co., 1953.

CLARK, MARK W. *From the Danube to the Yalu.* New York: Harper & Brothers, 1954.

DEAN, WILLIAM F. *The Dean Story.* New York: The Viking Press, 1954.

EISENHOWER, DWIGHT D. *Mandate for Change, 1953-1956.* New York: Doubleday & Co., 1963.

HULL, CORDELL, *The Memoirs of Cordell Hull.* 2 vols. New York: MacMillan, 1948.

LEAHY, WILLIAM. *I Was There.* New York: McGraw-Hill Book Co., 1950.

STETTINIUS, EDWARD R. *Roosevelt and the Russians, The Yalta Conference.* New York: Doubleday & Co., 1949.

STILWELL, JOSEPH W. *The Stilwell Papers.* New York: William Sloane Associates, Inc., 1948.

STIMSON, HENRY L. & MCGEORGE BUNDY. *On Active Service.* New York: Harper & Brothers, 1948.

TRUMAN, HARRY S. *Year of Decisions.* New York: Doubleday & Co., 1955.

*The Forrestal Diaries.* Walter Millis, ed. New York: The Viking Press, 1951.

YIM, LOUISE. *My Forty Years Fight for Korea.* New York: A. A. Wyn, 1951.


*Official Histories and Reports*

CLINE, RAY S. *Washington Command Post: The Operations Division,* The United States Army in World War II. Washington: Government Printing Office, 1951.

DEPARTMENT OF THE ARMY, OFFICE OF THE CHIEF OF MILITARY HISTORY. *Korea: 1950.* Washington: Government Printing Office, 1952.

GHQ, FAR EAST COMMAND. *Korea.* Hq XXIV Corps: Troop Information & Education Section, 1948.

MATLOFF, MAURICE & EDWIN M. SNELL. *Strategic Planning for Coalition Warfare, 1941-42,* The United States Army in World War II. Washington: Government Printing Office, 1958.

*Report of the United Nations Commission on the Unification and Rehabilitation of Korea,* General Assembly, Official Records: Eighteenth Session, Supplement No. 12 (A/551/2).

ROMANUS, CHARLES F. & RILEY SUNDERLAND. *Stilwell's Mission to China,* The United States Army in World War II. Washington: Government Printing Office, 1953.

STATE DEPARTMENT. *North Korea: A Case Study in the Techniques of Takeover.* Washington: Government Printing Office, 1961.

———. *A Historical Summary of United States-Korean Relations,* With a Chronology of Important Developments 1834-1962. Washington: Government Printing Office, 1962.

THE SECRETARIAT, SUPREME COUNCIL FOR NATIONAL RECONSTRUCTION. *Military Revolution in Korea.* Seoul: November 5, 1961.

THE SOUTH MANCHURIAN RAILWAY. *Second Report on Progress in Manchuria to 1930.* Dairen: 1931.


## UNPUBLISHED MANUSCRIPTS

"History of United States Army Forces in Korea," XXIV Corps Historical Section, n.d. Manuscript at Office of Chief of Military History, Washington.


## MAGAZINE ARTICLES

BRADLEY, OMAR N. "U.S. Military Policy:" 1950," *U.S. Army Combat Forces Journal,* October 1950.

———. "Strategy for Lasting Peace," *U.S. Army Combat Forces Journal,* May 1952.

FREYMOND, JACQUES. "Supervising Agreements: The Korean Experience," *Foreign Affairs,* April 1959.

GREY, ARTHUR L., JR. "The Thirty-Eighth Parallel," *Foreign Affairs,* April 1951.

HUPPERT, MAJ. G. H. "Korean Occupational Problems," *Military Review,* December 1949.

"Interview with Syngman Rhee," *U.S. News & World Report,* March 7, 1952.

LIMB, BEN C. "The Pacific Pact: Looking Forward or Backward," *Foreign Affairs,* July 1951.

MONAT, PAWEL. "Russians in Korea: The Hidden Bosses," *Life,* June 27, 1960.

RASTVOROV, YURI A. "Red Fraud and Intrigue in the Far East," *Life,* December 4, 1954.

WARNER, ALBERT L. "How the Korea Decision Was Made," *Harpers,* June 1951.


## NEWSPAPERS

*Current Digest of the Soviet Press,* Joint Committee of Slavic Studies, Vol. XIV, XV, 1962 & 1963.

*Izvestia, Pravda, Trud.* Soviet Press Translation. Seattle: Far Eastern Institute, University of Washington, 1946-53.

*Los Angeles Times.*
*Nippon Times*
*Pacific Stars & Stripes.*
*Philadelphia Inquirer.*
*Soviet News.* Published by the Press Department of the Soviet Embassy, London. Issues 1953-54.
*The New York Times*
*The New York Herald Tribune*
*Tokyo Mainichi*
*Washington Post*

## MISCELLANEOUS

*America's Future in the Pacific.* Lectures Delivered at the Second Quadrennial Institute, Mayling Soong Foundation, Wellesley College. New Brunswick: Rutgers University Press, 1947.
*Facts on File Yearbook, 1943,* Vol. III. New York: Person's Index, Facts on File, Inc., 1944.
———, *1946.* Vol. VI. New York: Person's Index, Facts on File, Inc., 1947.
*Korean Survey,* Vol. 4, No. 7. Washington: The Korean Research and Information Office, October 1955.
———, Vol. 10, No. 1. Washington: The Korean Research and Information Office, January 1961.
———, Vol. 1, No. 1. Washington: The Korean Research and Information Office, April 1961.
*Korean Report,* Vol. 1, No. 1. Washington: Korean Information Office, April 1961.
———, Vol. 1, No. 2. Washington: Korean Information Office, June 1961.
———, Vol. 1, No. 4. Washington: Korean Information Office, October 1961.
*Korea's Fight for Freedom, Selected Addresses by Korean Statesmen,* Vol. II. Washington: Korean Pacific Press, 1952.
*Pictorial Korea: 1951-1952.* International Publicity League of orea. Pusan, 1952.
*Supplement to New Korea,* No. 3 (Pyongyang), March 1958.
*The Korea Review.* Homer B. Hulbert, ed. Vol. IV, No. 1. Seoul: Methodist Publishing House, January 1904.
———. Vol. V, No. 7. Seoul: Methodist Publishing House, July 1905.

# Index

243

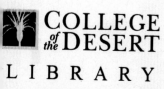